My Two Cents on Self-Love

A Compilation by Mistilei Wriston

My Two Cents on Self-Love

Campgroundtbd Publishing

Title: My Two Cents on Self-Love

Published by: Campgroundtbd Publishing

Compiled by: Mistilei Wriston

Graphics by: Nicole Angai-Galindo

Formatted by: Tara Christian

Description Mena, AR Campgroundtbd Publishing, [2023]

Paperback ISBN: 979-8-9878030-8-0

Hardback ISBN: 979-8-9878030-7-3

campgroundtbd@gmail.com

https://www.facebook.com/groups/quantumwriting300

This book is dedicated to my hero, Hayden Ray, and everything he taught the world

07/21/95-06/02/2023

Introduction from the compiler, Mistilei Wriston

In the late 90s, before I was introduced to the internet, I needed to raise money to take my highly disabled son to a specialist. I lived in a rural area outside a metroplex and had a mind for numbers. I did the calculations and realized that if everyone in that giant city would donate two cents, I would have enough without anyone going into debt.

With marker and poster board, I made a sign to this effect, taped photos of my son and the doctor, and headed off to the local grocery store with my baked goods in hand. My daughter and son were in the stroller, and we set up camp.

It started slow, people would buy a cookie, and some would leave a little extra change. As the cookies began to run low, someone came out with cookies they had purchased and donated them to our cause. Eventually, a local church that I didn't even attend donated baked goods for me to sell, and in a short time, I raised the funds.

This was a time when alternative medicine was very hush-hush and very expensive. It was also a time I was married with no idea where my husband was from day to day and desperately poor. I milked goats twice a day to provide the milk my son needed. It was a difficult time and somehow, those little donations from people allowed me to take him to the specialist and defy the medical community.

He not only lived past birth, past infancy, childhood, and puberty, but he also lived 10178 incredible days. He used each of them to teach me the value of the two cents worth in the smallest increments of joy.

As my life progressed, I spent a year traveling with a group of people called Tony Robbins Platinum Partnership for a year. It was expensive and exquisite and worth every cent. The lasting value in my life from the various people I met in the crowd at those events is a value beyond measure.

I decided to have a light summer. I wanted to do a small book on SELF-LOVE to release on the anniversary of my first solo compilation, *Here Comes the Sun*. I set the schedule carefully so my son and I could enjoy our first summer in our new, beautiful home in Western Arkansas.

He had other plans, and on June 2, 2023, on day 10178 as his mother, my son, my best friend, my confidant, and a young man I have been with 24/7 since the pandemic started, went to his next journey and shoved me through a funnel I thought I might somehow have avoided. I became a parent who lost a child.

I am so thankful my summer schedule was already light, so I can grieve and honor him at my pace. I am thankful I devoted two decades in life insurance and the past ten years to helping myself and others break cycles of pain. I know the steps. I am so grateful for the love and support of every author in this book that trusted me to deliver their incredible stories and this book to the world.

My son, Hayden Ray, built a warrior out of a broken little girl. He taught me to use my thoughts to change our world and to use writing to create my emotional reality. He taught this to everyone who crossed his path in some way or another. He taught us Hayden's Way. I will be an example of this for the duration.

Please know you are never alone, and it is my wish that you feel my love for you and this project. I have received such support since Hayden Ray passed that I can overflow into others—a gift I will cherish and respect.

With gratitude, we are all one,

Mistilei

#HAYDENSRAY #haydensway

Table of Contents

Ignite You and Live Your Best Life Now

By Craig Bruce

"You look awful!" the flight attendant said to me.

As I turned and stared at my reflection in that tiny airplane window, I suddenly felt tears welling up.

"Craig, you're a grown man crying in public! STOP crying! Your life sucks!"

But to everybody else, I was killing it! The truth was, I was killing myself!

I was at the top of my career, a partner in a Global Management Consulting Firm, an ex-pat in Brazil & Mexico, leading a line of business in Latin America, and consulting with clients across the Americas and Europe. I flew 2.5 million miles on one airline and one million miles on another.

I wore this lifestyle like it was a badge of honor! I even bragged about it to others. Yet, life as a global road warrior was taking its toll.

I'd wake up at 2 AM, my mind racing with no energy for the day. I struggled with my weight and pain in my entire body. And worst of all, this lifestyle was wrecking my relationships. I was running on that proverbial hamster wheel, and I couldn't jump off!

The day after that flight attendant made this grown man cry, I landed in the doctor's office. She ordered bed rest. But my version of bed rest was my laptop, cell phone,

1

and conference calls while pretending to rest in bed. I finally realized that my current lifestyle had become my "new normal," and it was killing me! Something had to change! I had to become an advocate for my own health and well-being!

In today's fast-paced world, I felt the stress of maintaining a busy and often chaotic lifestyle. Unfortunately, this overwhelming sense of "life fatigue" harmed my health, relationships, and career.

Although I didn't think it was attainable simultaneously, I wanted harmony within myself, my relationships, and my career. After living this global lifestyle, I learned that prioritizing ME determines long-term success in my career and personal relationships. Therefore, I was the common denominator in my life experiences.

Suddenly, it made sense to invest time in Me and love Me.

Loving myself was a journey of self-acceptance, intentional living, and prioritizing me. This led to a sense of fulfillment, authenticity, and a deep connection with my worth and well-being. I began embracing and nurturing my authentic self, clarifying my core values, and aligning my life with what truly mattered. It involved accepting and respecting myself, setting healthy boundaries, and making empowered decisions based on my values.

After retiring from my high-pressure career, I began a five-year journey researching science-backed solutions for the mind and body. My learnings became best practices I used to transform my life and the lives of my clients. Eight years later, I consistently make better food choices and feel confident in my body. I have more energy throughout the day and sleep like a baby at night.

And best of all, I now "honor space" for the relationships that matter. I believe health & lifestyle is a choice in winning at the game of life, relationships, and business and living my best life now. (I have included a sample of my day at the end of this chapter.)

I discovered that anyone could achieve even more success in their career without sacrificing their life and key relationships. Through coaching hundreds of high-performing business leaders and entrepreneurs, I found three key levers that are game changers for guiding high-performing leaders to even more success. These key levers:

- Consciousness
- Lifestyle
- Community

Consciousness is who I am being and how I show up daily. It involves growth, clarity, and intention. It is about identifying my top values and non-negotiables and using them as filters for all of my decisions—values include health, life partner, spouse, kids, grandkids, or career.

I asked myself three questions.

- What are my top 3 values?
- Who do I want to BE?
- Why is all this important to me?

Then, I created an I AM Statement to guide my journey. "I am the CEO of my life, living my life through my values of Connection to Source, Health & Wellness, Long-term Relationships, and Diversity & Inclusion while empowering others to embrace their uniqueness and soar in all aspects of their life!" Now, I wake up to this version of self-love every day.

Lifestyle is how I live to support my mind and body for wellness and longevity. Focusing on how I nourish, restore (sleep!), and move my body are key components to IGNITE ME!

I adopted science-backed behaviors like:

- Hydrate before I caffeinate.

- Wake up at the same time daily and get at least 15 minutes of sunlight and movement.

- End all caffeine by early afternoon.

- Shut off all electronics at least 30 minutes before lights out.

Community is the tribe of people I interact with daily. It is where I belong, can be authentic, and where I give and receive accountability and support so that we co-create together. My communities are key for preventing feelings of loneliness and isolation. Yet, being part of a community requires being very clear about how I interact with and how my community interacts with me. That means setting and communicating my *"terms of engagement"* (aka boundaries) so that others know what's important to ME. Thus, empowering ME to take back control.

My four best practices for creating my *"terms of engagement"* are:

4

- Identify my top 3 values & non-negotiables.
- Scan my environment to identify where values and non-negotiables are being infringed upon and derailing me.
- Develop an action plan to address when I get derailed.
- Communicate, communicate, and communicate my terms of engagement to my community.

Creating a life that IGNITES me involves focusing on my consciousness, lifestyle, and community. The adventure of self-love embodies strength, resilience, and a commitment to ME.

I unlocked my true potential by harmonizing business, personal life, and relationships, embracing individuality, empowering others, and promoting an authentic and supportive environment. I was ready to step into my fullest being as a human. I was ready to be truly fulfilled and aligned with the key values of my life.

Even the smallest steps shifted my life and health in ways I never dreamed possible!

Here is my morning ritual loaded with science-backed behaviors designed to set me up for success throughout the day.

5 AM – Wake up and get connected to my Source through meditation

5:30 AM -- Drink 16oz of water, walk outside to connect to the earth, and set daily intentions by asking myself:

- How am I going to show up today?

- What is my focus today to get me closer to my goals?
- What am I grateful for today?

6 AM - 7:30 AM -- Movement/mobility / aerobic capacity (4 - 5 days/week)

7:30 AM - 8 AM -- Shower, get dressed, and nourish the body with food

8 AM -- Begin work

11 AM - 11:15 AM -- Morning break to breathe and reflect (alarm set for a reminder)

1 PM - 2 PM -- Lunch with no electronics

I invite you to take a moment and reflect on how a morning ritual might set you up for success throughout your day and how it demonstrates loving YOU!

Here is my evening ritual loaded with science-backed behaviors and designed to "protect" my last hour before bedtime so that I get quality deep and REM sleep.

6 PM -- Stop work and shut down laptop (alarm set for a reminder)

6 PM - 7 PM -- Dinner (no electronics)

8 PM – 8:30 PM – Shut off all electronics and put on blue light-blocking glasses

8:30 PM - 9 PM -- Wind-down time to reflect on the day, breathe and stretch lightly

9 PM -- Lights out

Again, I invite you to take a moment and reflect on how an evening ritual might set you up for a night of quality sleep and prepare you for success the next day.

Craig Bruce is a former burned-out global executive who struggled with exhaustion, poor sleep, inconsistent food choices, and feeling confident in his own skin. Now, as a High-Performance Lifestyle Consultant, he guides other high-performing business leaders & entrepreneurs to achieve even more success in their careers without sacrificing their life and key personal relationships.

He is an international speaker with an MBA from Vanderbilt University and a business degree from UNC-Chapel Hill. He is a former partner at Hewitt Associates for 25 years and lived internationally for over five years. He also worked as a Health Coach & Educator for the Equinox Sports Club Los Angeles. In addition, Craig has partnered with hundreds of clients to achieve even more success and live their best life now.

Craig believes owning your health & lifestyle is a CHOICE to win at the game of life & business!

To set up a complimentary Ignite You call with Craig

https://go.oncehub.com/callwithcraig

To Join the Ignite You Facebook Community

www.facebook.com/groups/evolvehealth/

To connect with Craig on social media

http://linkedin.com/in/craig-bruce-b44766146

https://www.facebook.com/Evolve-Health-and-Lifestyle-107654944564923

https://www.Instagram.com/craig.bruce.140

Personal Responsibility and Self Love

By Julia Caton

There became a moment in life where I began to recognize I had sold myself to the things, the people, and the circumstances I wanted to acquire or associate with. What was the cost of such a diminishing pursuit? Did I sacrifice the clarity of mental and emotional well-being? How about the loss of financial or physical health? Did the price cause me to question my value and self-worth, or perhaps a better question, did I lose my identity of self when I poured too much into that "desired outcome" without any agreements of reciprocation or reparations from those other people, circumstances, or things? My answer is, "Absolutely, unequivocally, yes to all of the above."

A huge revelation was realizing I had made a one-sided, unconscious agreement with every man I dated. They were completely unaware of the expectational requirements I had lined up for them. Sadly neither did I until very recently. Ironically when things fell apart, which they inevitably did, I had someone else to blame, judge, or distract me from having to claim ownership of the impending pain. GOD, THE PAIN, SO MUCH PAIN.... Taking a personal responsibility inventory was one of the most painful, brutal, and beautiful gifts I chose to give myself. The mantra for today is, "Hi, my name is Julia. I am a very active co-dependent and have chosen sobriety." This is my two cents on self-love and the reason I write the following":

Just For Today

Just for today, I choose to remove myself from the person, place, or circumstance that has me bound in shackles.

Just for today, I accept the responsibility for putting on the shackles and then chose to stay there.

Just for today, I will resist the urge to text, call or visit the source of my drug.

Just for today, I recognize the word "drugs" is a simple code for anything or anyone I am addicted to in my life.

Just for today, I have chosen to resist spending money or eating chocolate to temporarily ease the suffering of my heart.

Just for today, I choose to savor every aspect of the drink or food I consume.

Just for today, I give myself permission to enjoy the taste, texture, and timing of food consumption.

Just for today, I choose a walk over worry; I am pausing, wondering why that person hasn't reached out to me.

Just for today, I have decided to get dressed when the sun rises instead of lying in bed until noon.

Just for today, and today only, I give myself the opportunity lay on my living room floor crumpled and crying until the sobbing stops.

Just for today, I encourage myself to smile from the depths of my being – let my joy spring flow.

Just for today, I am choosing to take as many breaths as I need to remind myself, I am still alive.

Just for today, I grant my feet the freedom to feel the bare earth beneath them.

Just for today, I allow myself to be angry over the tiniest things or the largest challenges.

Just for today, even as I allow myself the compassion to understand that the tiniest things or the largest challenges were never the real sources of my anger, frustration, or pain.

Just for today, I encourage myself to tend to my broken heart in the most gentle and gracious ways.

Just for today, I will tell myself it is time to get my ass moving- it starts with a single action.

Just for today, I yield myself to what is versus what I thought was.

Just for today, I agree to let all the pain come forward so that I might be present with it today in exchange for the peace of tomorrow.

Just for today, I have chosen to attempt to make amends to one person I have harmed in my life.

Just for today, I evaluate my options and choose the path that best honors my inner values.

Just for today, I choose boundaries over bulldozing another into showing up, aligning with me, or choosing me.

Just for today, I will say yes.

Just for today, I hold my hand over my heart, apologize to the one I have hurt the most, lied to constantly more than another, and sacrificed at will – myself.

Just for today, I admit my faults and choose to love all that I am from a place of gratitude and forgiveness... ALL that I am.

Just for today, I hold a space to love without reservation or manipulation for the sake of love alone.

Just for today, I give myself permission to feel everything that shows up as it shows up and when it shows up.

Just for today, I choose to save myself.

Just for today, I am choosing to allow myself to be loved on, covered by, and adored by my puppies.

Just for today, I will feel the sun on every aspect of my skin, from cheekbones to bum cheeks, with gratitude, freedom, and child-like abandonment.

Just for today, I will only be where I am celebrated – I do not accept the concept of being tolerated.

Just for today, I will say no.

Just for today, I will keep the commitments I have made for myself.

Just for today, I will honor the commitments I have made to others.

Just for today, I will offer forgiveness, compassion, and empathy toward everything that I want to resist.

Just for today, I will make amends and apologize for where I have caused harm to another.

Just for today, I will write my thoughts instead of speaking without thinking – let me be wiser in my walk forward.

Just for today, I will celebrate life and my survival rate of 100% of everything I have experienced.

Just for today, I will accept responsibility for everything, everyone, and every aspect that has been a part of the orchestration of my life. I am the common denominator in it all.

Just for today, I pause, feel the breeze on my skin, play footies with the blades of grass, and hear the messages of the wilderness around me.

Just for today, I admit and remind myself to be present.

Just FOR TODAY...

I thought addictions were different. Depending on the circumstances, each one had to be overcome and addressed in some magical formula or rehab presentation. I even idealized some were better than others. Let me state clearly and definitively, an addiction is an addiction. To think my co-dependency addiction trumps food, alcoholism, working out, shopping, sex or chocolate addictions is another lie I told myself to distract me from doing my inner work. Addictions are, at their very core, simply a desire and dependency on a drug formed internally or provided externally. I now hold the opinion that there are unlimited capacities to which one can be addicted.

Perhaps, that is one of the many faces of self-love. It permits us and invites us to dive deep into our most inner being, to discover the bounty, bliss, and beauty of doing our own work. Self-love is admitting we need to take a different path; not everyone will love us or have our best interests at heart. Self-love is being willing to say goodbye, offer a salutation, grant praise, or apologize when warranted. Self-love is the recognition of our humanity. Self-love is admitting that even when doing our best, we will mess up, fail, or falter. Self-love is holding a space for celebrating that every aspect of existence is precious and occurring for us. Understanding the whole of our capacity, every high and every low creates the possibilities for making and being human spectacular.

For me, coming to the mountain retreat and staying a Campgroundtbd for all of May 2023, choosing to face what I had been running from, to come to terms with the truths my inner being and external support team had been telling me, and to choose to save myself, was and is, one of the greatest gifts of self-love I can give myself. "Just for today," my daily mantra... I am choosing to stay when I want to run, feel all the pain when I want to numb, and learn to self-soothe, scream out loud or write my way through it all. This is my two cents on self-love.

Julia, a two-time international and three-time US and Canada bestselling author has spent the last ten years focusing on mental health, well-being, and spiritual and ministerial guidance. Julia has an undergraduate degree in Human Development and a graduate degree in Human Relations focusing on Clinical Mental Health. Julia has numerous coaching specialty certifications and a successful therapeutic coaching ministry. Currently, Julia is exploring writing and publishing opportunities with Campgroundtbd Publishing, and is the smiling co-host with the feminine perspective on the podcast, The Coached Soul with Steve Hudgins.

Your mental health matters – If you are looking for a methodology process with a whole-being perspective on healing, reach out to 918CoachJulia.

TicTok @juliaicaton

918coach.com

LinkedIn www.linkedin.com/in/juliaca

We're in this Together

By Kym Luck

My thoughts and words are a bit scattered and messy right now. I've just been through a 9-month emotional tornado that ended a week ago. I've been on a journey intertwined with exploring self-love and the diverse archetypes of womanhood. Within this chapter of my life, I invite you to delve into my personal narrative as I navigate the intricate path of self-discovery and love.

Tall, Dark, and Handsome (TDH) entered our life, stirring a connection that resonated deeply with the Lover archetype within us. Our heart was liberated from the shackles of solitude. After four years of embracing independence and reveling in solitude, we felt ready to embark on a journey of love—an enduring and fulfilling love. TDH was not a stranger; we had known him as a family friend for years. We believed he was forging through his own journey of loss, as a widower of 2 years. Our laughter flowed effortlessly, and a foundation of trust was swiftly established.

You may find the use of "us," "we," and "our" perplexing. Through these pronouns, I acknowledge the mosaic of archetypes that reside within me—the Lover, the Maiden, the Sage, the Queen, the Mother, and the Mystic. Each archetype represents a distinct facet of my womanhood, offering unique perspectives and wisdom throughout the various chapters of my life. Through my journey with TDH, the strength of my self-love would face a challenging test.

16

TDH and the Maiden ventured into the Wild West, exploring the magnificence of national parks, hiking through breathtaking landscapes, and racing Razors across the rugged terrain. We would stargaze. He would sing to me as I lay on his lap, snuggled against his warm body. He was gentle, kind, and aimed to please. As our connection deepened, TDH merged into the fabric of my life, physically moving into my small living space without a formal invitation. The lines between his existence and mine began to blur. It was difficult for me to lose the long stretches of solitude I was accustomed to. Parts of me were content with the attention, and others felt smothered. When I tried to communicate this need for balance, he thought I was pushing him away, and we would end up in a senseless conflict.

Money and alcohol soon became complicated subjects, as the Mother within me felt compelled to help the little boy within him navigate the challenges of civilian life. I experienced a conflicting mix of frustration and a sense of responsibility for his life experience.

Within the labyrinth of this complex relationship, the once-sturdy boundaries I had painstakingly crafted for myself began to crumble. The enticing allure of the Lover archetype blinded me to the warning signs, compelling me to compromise my authenticity and neglect self-care. I found myself making excuses for TDH's questionable behavior, silencing the voice of my inner truth. The serenity that had once enveloped my soul dissipated as TDH's stagnant energy infiltrated my space, depriving me of the life-giving air that had once filled the room. Neglecting my own self-care, I accommodated his neediness at the expense of my well-being. My inner peace slipped away as he expressed his feelings of inadequacy in the presence of my multidimensional character. I began to contort my behavior in an attempt to make the relationship better.

The vibrant energy that had once fueled my existence seemed to wane, overpowered by TDH's passive nature. He was a passenger in my world. I became the source of his excitement, his security blanket. Terms of endearment—love, sweetie, babe—slipped effortlessly from his lips, yet their utterance masked a shallow understanding of my true essence. At one point, I asked him to write a romantic note to me each day, allowing him to express his emotions and share his joy in joining me on my adventures. The notes were about his feelings and needs and nothing about me. An emotional harpoon pierced the buoyancy of my vibrant, joy-filled life. I found myself tethered to a dark, heavy stone. With each tug of the harpoon's string, my elevated existence plummeted, unable to counterbalance the weight of his unenlightened presence.

The Sage within me emerged from her respite, her wisdom piercing through the fog that had clouded my perception. I realized that TDH had pressed the "pause" button on his grief journey when his wife fell ill, only to resume it upon entering my life. His rules were based on his 30-year marriage, and he manipulated our relationship to resemble his old life. His outdated beliefs and behaviors had nothing to do with me— his unfinished emotional work that hindered our connection. The Sage informed the Lover that this man did not genuinely love me. He had used me as if I were a fueling station and drained away all of my energy. I was exhausted, listless, disappointed, and suffering. My addiction to attention was compromising my life.

The words of Tony Robbins reverberated within me as I contemplated the power of relationships: "*The quality of our life is the quality of our relationships.*" These words echoed through the chambers of my soul, reminding me of the power I possessed to shape the course of my own life through the choices I made. The regal presence of the Queen archetype within me stepped forward, reclaiming control over the narrative of my existence. With the imminent start of a demanding summer business, where my Warrior Goddess Queen reigns supreme, I could no longer tolerate the intrusion of such nonsense from this interloper.

Resolute and unwavering, the Queen delivered the message that TDH could no longer be a part of my life. He attempted to bribe his way back into my world, offering assistance in my business endeavors while hoping to avoid confronting his own lack of independence. The Queen remained unaffected by such enticements. She severed the strings of the harpoon, cutting the ties that bound us, and I ascended to my normal altitude—liberated and unburdened.

Reflecting on my past relationship, it was apparent that our relationship was strained and marked by low-vibration behaviors. Arguments became frequent, and the energy between us felt heavy and burdensome. His lack of effective communication skills exacerbated the tension, making it challenging to address our issues and find common ground.

I now recognize that we had very little in common. Our interests, values, and aspirations diverged significantly, leading to disconnection and a constant feeling of being out of sync. Our union felt forced and lacked the natural ease and compatibility that should accompany a fulfilling partnership.

The awkwardness that permeated our relationship served as a constant reminder that something was amiss. It stood in stark contrast to the genuine connections and harmonious relationships I had experienced in the past. Despite my efforts to navigate these challenges and seek resolution, it became clear that the foundation of our union was shaky and unsustainable.

While the journey was undoubtedly challenging, I consider it a valuable learning experience. It taught me the importance of alignment and compatibility in relationships and the significance of effective communication and shared values. It reminded me to trust my instincts and prioritize my well-being and happiness. All of the parts in me have a valuable voice. I love that the Lover was willing to take a chance on love. I honor the Maiden for her wild, adventurous spirit and ability to share that with someone on a whim. I am grateful for the Mother in me, for she has a caring and compassionate heart. I appreciate the wisdom of the Sage that keeps her eyes and ears open as the keeper of our knowledge and lessons learned. I admire the Mystic and her never-ending pursuit of spiritual growth. Above all, I am extremely grateful for the strength and confidence of the Queen in me. She is our courageous leader and does not hesitate when it's time to make the best choice for our best life and our best self. In a world that often emphasizes external validation and comparison, self-love (of all our selves) serves as a guiding light towards genuine, juicy happiness and fulfillment.

Kym Luck is a dynamic entrepreneur, author, and licensed Equine Gestalt Therapist. As the proud owner of Vail Stables, a Top 150 Mom & Pop Business recognized by Entrepreneur Magazine, she has carved a niche for herself in the business world.

Beyond her business accomplishments Kym has made waves in the literary world as a #1 Amazon International Best-Selling author. Collaborating with Mistilei Wriston and Campgroundtbd Publishing, she has shared her experiences and insights with readers worldwide.

As a licensed Equine Gestalt Therapist, Kym merges her love for horses with her desire to help others. Using horses as partners in therapy, she facilitates healing and personal growth for individuals and corporations alike. Through this unique approach, Kym empowers her clients to develop essential life skills, unlock their potential, and find inner harmony.

Outside of her professional pursuits, she embraces life with boundless energy and a thirst for adventure.

Riding her horses in team roping events and embarking on scuba diving escapades in exotic locations are among her favorite pastimes. Her adventurous spirit and determination are a testament to her unwavering commitment to pursuing what truly resonates with her.

https://www.facebook.com/kym.luck/

IG: @kymknowswhy

IG @vailstables

Defying Despair

By Becky Blake

Unlock Your Superpower
Unleash Your Life

In the tumultuous year of 1994, my life seemed to crumble around me, again. I grappled with the demands of raising newborn twin boys and my 16-month-old daughter alone, all three with unique needs including Autism, brain injury, intellectual disability, social, sensory, speech issues, and defiance. As if that wasn't enough, the chaos was compounded by a painful divorce. Despair cast its heavy shadow over my heart, and I yearned for a glimmer of hope to guide me through this storm.

During this time of profound darkness, I stumbled upon a small bookstore, seeking solace within the pages of a book. As if guided by an unseen hand, my eyes fell upon a book that would alter the course of my life and the lives of my children, my family, and all those I would eventually touch. Its title beckoned me with an air of possibility—"Awaken the Giant Within" by Tony Robbins.

Curiosity piqued, I reached out and held the book in my hands, its weight symbolizing the transformative journey that awaited me. Little did I know that within those pages lay the keys to unlocking the power within, the tools to design the life of my dreams, and the wisdom to help my children and others navigate their unique challenges.

I immersed myself in Tony Robbins' teachings, devouring his words with an insatiable hunger for change.

Through his guidance, I discovered the immense power of belief, the importance of setting outcomes, that taking action is power, and so much more. Armed with these newfound tools, I began to chart a course toward a brighter future for myself and my children.

The years passed, and my commitment to personal growth remained unwavering. One of my future outcomes was to attend one of Tony's live events in Fiji. Finally, the day arrived when I found myself standing in the welcoming embrace of Fiji, surrounded by the love and joy of the beautiful Fijian people at Tony's resort.

As the event unfolded, I listened intently to Tony's words, his wisdom resonating deep within my being. Then, in a serendipitous encounter, I joined his elite personal development group, Platinum Partners, and came face to face with Tony Robbins himself. Overwhelmed by gratitude, I seized the opportunity to share my story with him—a moment that would forever inspire both of us.

Tears streamed down Tony's face as he listened, deeply moved by the profound impact his teachings had on saving my life and the transformative effect they had on my children. He was genuinely touched by the program I had created, a heartfelt endeavor aimed at not only helping children overcome Autism, as well as children with a range of other challenging brain and behavioral differences. In that sacred moment, I realized that our connection extended beyond the realm of mentorship—it was a profound exchange of gratitude and healing.

A few years later, as Tony wrote his book "Unshakable," I had the opportunity to show him my innovative techniques for detoxing. He especially liked my

C-spine technique. As I explained the process and its profound potential for healing, I noticed a spark of intrigue in his eyes. At that moment, Tony's mind swiftly grasped the immense possibilities of what I had to offer, reinforcing our connection beyond mentorship—it was a meeting of minds driven by a shared purpose.

In the following years, I dedicated myself to sharing the knowledge and techniques that had set me free. Armed with Tony's teachings, I embarked on a global mission, traveling from one corner of the world to another, sharing my expertise with families in their homes, guiding schools in implementing effective strategies, and impacting countless lives.

While working in homes and schools, I witnessed children with autism breaking free from the confines of their challenges. Nonverbal children found their voices, unlocking a world of communication and connection. My program allowed us to shed light on the misunderstood, celebrating the progress made by those initially deemed defiant or brain injured. Moreover, it emphasized the importance of embracing the uniqueness of ourselves and our children. Children achieved significant milestones. From potty training to reading skills, I empowered them to become leaders in their own right, fostering their personal growth and development.

With each triumph, I celebrated the resilience of the human spirit, our human superpower. And as I witnessed the ripple effect of my work, the impact reverberating through the lives of countless families, I realized the true essence of self-love.

My chapters were still unfolding. One beautiful day at the fairgrounds, where the exhilarating atmosphere filled the air, I stood alongside a group of moms. My heart beat with anticipation as my son prepared to race in the thrilling Supermoto dirtbike event. Anxiously, I awaited the race's start and finish, my mind consumed with worry for my son's safety.

As the race unfolded before my eyes, I watched in awe and trepidation as my son and dirtbike soared through the air, defying gravity with his daring maneuvers. However, my joy quickly turned to panic as I witnessed only his body fly through the air and crash to the ground with a jarring impact. Fear gripped my heart as I rushed to his side, only to discover that he wasn't breathing. With a sense of urgency, we swiftly transported him across the street to the hospital, where the grim reality unfolded before us. The doctors informed me that my son had suffered a broken neck, another severe brain injury and had been clinically dead for three agonizing minutes. As I absorbed this devastating news, I felt a chilling sense of déjà vu. It echoed the words I had heard years ago when he was just two and a half years old, a proclamation that he was brain-injured and may never achieve anything significant, perhaps even requiring institutional care. This was the same time I had first found Tony's book. What I had just gone through, for 14 years, had been training for this very moment.

In the face of profound adversity, the true essence of self-love revealed itself. I came to understand that self-love is not solely about weathering life's storms; it is about thriving amidst the chaos and embracing the understanding that within every tragedy lies a hidden gift,

26

a profound lesson yearning to be learned. It is an unwavering belief that we inherently deserve love, happiness, and fulfillment regardless of our circumstances.

Through my experiences, I have learned that there is a gift, a silver lining, and a light at the end of the tunnel after our struggles—if we choose to look. After supporting my son through his recovery and implementing my brain program with him, I witnessed the remarkable healing of his brain. His thought patterns, word recognition, self-esteem, and confidence were restored.

Self-love is about living life with childlike curiosity, eagerly anticipating each day's wonders. It is about finding joy in the simplest things, in the gentle touch of a loved one, in the vibrant colors of a sunset, and in a child's laughter. Through this lens of wonder, I rediscover the beauty that surrounds me, even in the darkest of times.

The path has not always been easy, and there are moments when doubt and despair threaten to consume me once again. During my latest dark night of the soul period, in the wake of my mother's unexpected death, the death of my sister, my dad and the suicide of my best friend, my family's rejection at my mom's funeral, my brother's cruelty, and the halt of my lifestyle, business and working live Tony events - I found myself teetering on the edge of deep despair. The weight of grief, loss, and betrayal bore down on me, suffocating my spirit. Desperate for solace, thinking back to the last time I was truly happy, I turned to the familiar embrace of a live, in-person Tony Robbins event again as a Platinum Partner.

As I entered the room, my eyes were drawn to Tony, and I noticed something too familiar—his ears were red, a telltale sign of stress and overwhelm. An unexplainable connection stirred within me, a deep-seated knowing that I had a gift to offer, just as Tony had gifted me with his wisdom.

Driven by a potent mix of courage and compassion, I approached Tony, reminding him of my C-spine technique that had brought healing and solace to so many. Then, with gentle words and hands, I guided him back to a calm state, rekindling his self-healing abilities. At that moment, a full circle was completed, an exchange of healing and support, mentee to mentor—the truest gift.

Encouraged by this newfound courage, I stood before everyone, my voice trembling with vulnerability. With unwavering conviction, I shared my journey, of how Tony saved my life not once but twice, the impact he's had on my children and family, as well as the depths of my despair, the transformative impact of his teachings, and the profound gratitude I felt for his guidance.

As my words echoed through the room, a palpable shift occurred. Hearts opened, tears flowed, and the community formed—a tribe of individuals united by the understanding that self-love was the key to unlocking our greatest potential. Self-Love allows us to Defy Despair.

Perhaps the most profound lesson I have learned is that self-love is not an isolated endeavor—it thrives in community, connection, and collaboration. Through our shared experiences and collective support, we create a tapestry of love and

28

understanding, weaving together the fabric of a more compassionate and inclusive world.

As I stand on the precipice of each new chapter, I am filled with gratitude for the experiences that have shaped me, the mentors who have guided me, and the unwavering belief that self-love is the foundation upon which dreams are built.

And so, dear reader, as I look back on my extraordinary journey, I am humbled by the realization that self-love is the beacon that guides us through the storms of life. The inner compass leads us to our most authentic selves, allowing us to navigate the depths of despair and emerge stronger, wiser, and more compassionate.

May you remain grounded in the understanding that self-love is not a destination but an ongoing practice— a daily commitment to nurture and honor oneself. For within you lies a giant, waiting to be awakened, waiting to conquer the world with curiosity, happy anticipation, and true understanding.

May you embark on your voyage of self-love, and may it lead you to the life of your dreams—a life brimming with joy, resilience, and the unwavering knowledge that you are worthy of all the love and fulfillment the universe has to offer.

As I bid you farewell, remember this: You are the hero of your own story, and within you lies the strength to overcome any challenge, the wisdom to navigate any storm, and the capacity to create a life of meaning and purpose. So awaken your giant within, unleash your life, and embrace your uniqueness and gifts. You are the hero of your own story, and within you lies the strength to overcome any challenge lies within you. You are the GIANT.

I am also reminded I am the hero of my own story, and within me lies the strength to overcome any challenge. I am the Giant!

This picture, of me and Tony, is the exact moment I came full circle, January 2022, as I was reminding him of my C-Spine technique.

Becky Blake, author, speaker, brain specialist, and dedicated mother, has made an indelible mark in the realm of child development. Through her tireless efforts, she propelled her own three children beyond the confines of Autism, brain injury, and social, sensory & speech challenges. Her paradigm-shifting approach has helped thousands live more compelling lives.

Often compared to a real-life Mary Poppins, Becky's groundbreaking enterprise, **CreatingSuperKids.com**, has become a sought-after resource for parents &

professionals striving to provide the best for their children. Her #1 best-selling book, "***Unlock Your Child's True Potential***," offers hope & guidance to understanding the misunderstood.

Driven by her commitment to revolutionize medicine & education, a PhDc in Psychoneurology, she stands at the forefront of innovation, developing AI apps, online training programs, & has a groundbreaking school program, bringing transformative knowledge to educational institutions worldwide. Professionals call her expertise the holy grail of healing, witnessing the profound impact she continues to make in homes & schools across the globe.

TV special explaining what I do

https://youtu.be/NwBTXgw-Hl4

Case Study with pictures

https://behaviorrevolution.com/testimonials/

UNLOCK YOUR CHILD'S TRUE POTENTIAL book, Breakthrough Social, Sensory, Speech, Behavior Barriers

https://a.co/d/5cOXcww

To set up a call fill out this

https://behaviorrevolution.com/contact/

Helping families better understand their child in order to best help create major results

www.BehaviorRevolution.com

Returning to the Authentic Me

By Susannah Dawn

"I'm not what I used to be, yet I am who
I've always been."

There was a little girl who loved life. She was energetic, confident, and enjoyed playing with the other kids, especially two girls, her best friends at school. And, like any girl, she loved to sneak into her mom's closet to play dress-up. She loved thinking about the clothes she would wear as she got older. She knew who she was, enjoyed life, and was very loving and outgoing to her friends.

One day, however, her world crashed down around her. It was the day her father first caught her playing dress-up. The anger that exuded from him was unexpected. As he proceeded to spank her for her as yet unknown transgression, her father's wrath only grew. The fear she felt growing inside kept her from asking him why he was mad. She could only wonder what she did wrong.

It was by no means her first spanking. However, all of the previous ones she knew she deserved... accepting the momentary pain as she promised to do better. This time... it would take a handful more such encounters with her dad before she got the painful – yet never verbally spoken – message: never get caught playing dress-up.

Though she knew who she was, it became clear she needed to hide that knowledge from her father, followed by her friends, and then the world. She realized how she had to pretend to be something she was not to avoid the punishment she began to receive that first day... when she was only seven years old... and hid her true self in a dark place.

The thing is... this is a true story... my story. That was the day my dad first rejected me because I wasn't what he expected. He could only view me based on my shell, the physical box into which I was born. The problem was that my body failed to align with my soul, something he still cannot accept today.

Sure, some may say I was born into the wrong body, even going as far as to say God made a mistake... though that's not how I see it. My soul is female, a fact I knew by age three when I prayed every night to wake up a girl. So while God placed me in this shell, He did not make a mistake. God never makes mistakes. He put me on this world, at this time, for a reason. He knew it was an age when the body could be aligned to my soul because, unlike my shell, my soul, my authentic self, which cannot be changed.

And while this may be my story, many in the world have similar stories. I hid my authentic self for a half-century. Other people hide aspects of their true selves for similar reasons: being neurodiverse, having a non-regional accent, being LGBTQ+, and so many other traits they hide for fear of what others might say or do to them. They hide, even when those attributes are only a small piece of who they are as a whole.

Having to hide who I was made it difficult to love who I was or practice any type of self-love for most of my life. Growing up in a house where my dad constantly teased and ridiculed me was difficult, especially when his comments were not specifically aimed at me but designed to fall around and affect me like artillery shells. The tone and emotions embedded in his words had his desired effect, or so he thought. The actual result was me doing everything I could to hide my true self in order to identify as what I wasn't – a shell that spoke "boy" to those who saw it. By the time I graduated high school, I had no self-confidence, self-esteem, or hope.

The only place I could safely be my authentic self was in the darkness of my own box. Inside, fear held me trapped, seductively speaking to me using words like grains of truth woven into its lies. If I looked through the cracks in the walls of the box, fear warned me that I was likely to be physically harmed… or probably worse. When I looked out, I failed to see the translucent web of its lies because I only saw the green spouts from the seeds of truth it planted. Every place I worked, I spent energy hiding. I didn't make friends for the same reason. A real friend is someone you share with, open up and let them know your bad as well as good, knowing they are there for you unconditionally. However, if they learn I'm _____, the fear is of more painful rejection, which I'd already gone through with my family. There was no need to pick at scabs or old wounds.

For five decades I did nothing for myself, certainly nothing that could be considered self-love, due to the constant repression of the girl I am, in order to survive. I did the things men were supposed to do, became an Army Cavalry officer, joined men's groups in church, and maintained a stoic appearance in most places with people. I even blocked the memories of my childhood days, blotting out the time when I was free and played with my friends. Yet, no matter what I did, I was not happy, including becoming divorced after almost two decades of marriage.

However, a handful of years ago, light began to shine into my dark box. It was the light of awareness. As it grew, it's glow began to surround me, and in doing so, forced the darkness where my fears lived to shrink. I began to think more about who I was... and about who I've always been. That spark continued to grow, slowly, until a new catalyst ignited new life into it.

It was the day after Christmas 2019. I walked into a major cosmetics store with the idea of quietly buying a foundation to play with... taking the first step in doing something for me. The beauty advisor I spoke with kept my attention focused on her as she asked questions. As she put products on my face, she helped me take the first public steps to being my authentic self, carefully stepping outside of my dark box.

Over the next year, the box I had hidden in for so long went through its own transformation. It slowly metamorphosed from a sterile box to a magical cocoon. It carried me along with it, taking me to the beginning of my own reinvention process. Every day I would step outside, into the world, as my authentic self. My only social contacts were during my visits to the cosmetic store, where everyone quickly knew me, knew my story, and accepted me unconditionally.

Through this process, I began to feel love for the person I saw in the mirror, something I hadn't felt in a half-century. The more I stepped out as who I was at my core, the more the walls crumbled that I had been hiding behind for most of my life... protecting me from a world I feared would harm me because of my truth.

What I found was what amounted to a miracle. As I spent my days walking in public as my authentic self, more amazing things happened. It began with my friends in the major cosmetic store who took me under their wings as one of them. They helped me with skincare, makeup, and my hair to the point they began asking me for advice. My sense of fashion blossomed at the same time, and soon I was able to fully love the woman I saw in the mirror every day. All of this was the foundation for taking care of myself, giving myself the self-love I'd been missing all my life. What I was doing showed me how I believed in my own self-worth... value... meaning... in this world. And it was all due to living as who I was created to be at my core – letting my female soul live free.

In doing so, I lived and engaged with others as my authentic self. Even a year earlier it would have been impossible to consider. However, to get as far as I did – and so quickly – was due to a key step in my journey of self-love: I owned my fears, thereby taking away the control they held over me for oh so much of my life. What many don't realize is how, when we own our fears, they no longer own us... they no longer pull the strings that kept us stuck in boxes.

It must also be understood how fear lies to us. It carefully weaves that grain of truth within the web of its lies, so we'll only focus on it. In that way, when we look beyond the box we're kept in, we fail to see those seedlings for the red herring they are... fail to realize how fear's lies are holding us back.

Once I owned my fear, a new world of confidence opened up. Instead of fearing what might happen if someone found out about my truth, I took control of my situation. It became my decision regarding who I told my story to... telling them what I was willing to let them know, when / where I wanted to open up, how I wanted to let them know, why I felt like telling them... and most importantly, IF I wanted to tell them.

It also meant I refused to be defined by the boxes others put me in – the labels placed on me, or the ones I crawled into because my fear told me to. I was able to forgive both others who hurt me, and the hurt I caused myself due to hiding so long. I was able to remove the weight of the past off my shoulders and thereby live in the present. When letting go of the pains we let fester inside of us from guilt, shame, anger, abuse, and so many other events from our past, it's like stepping out of a smoke-filled room and breathing fresh air.

It took five decades for that little girl to step out into the world after that first encounter with her dad. However, once I stepped into the open as my authentic self, I was finally able to give and receive the self-love I'd been missing all my life. Being authentic was critical to improving my life and being who I was always meant to be in this world.

Returning to the Authentic Me
By Susannah Dawn

"I'm not what I used to be, yet I am who I've always been." - Susannah Dawn

---

Susannah Dawn entered 2022 with a total reinvention and now looks at life and business from a vantage point set beyond labels... beyond boxes... those places in which our fears work hard to confine us, as they try to keep us from seeing how we are so much more than boxes and labels could ever express.

A motivational speaker, storyteller, and business consultant, Susannah Dawn no longer fits the proverbial box – and never did. She speaks at length on the importance of being our authentic selves and how to turn the obstacles of pivoting – of reinvention, into speed bumps. Susannah works with women, groups, and organizations as they consider their own reinvention processes so they, too, can move beyond boxes and labels.

LinkedIn: linkedin.com/in/susannah-dawn-freelance-writer

Website: SusannahDawnWriter.com

Busy Loving Myself

By Yvette Jones

I was having a heart attack. I was at my fiance's house when I felt a deep sharp pain in my left arm and down the left side of my back. I tried everything to relieve that pain. I took a hot bath, did some push-ups, and stretched my arms. Nothing worked. I never thought it was a heart attack. And yet, I found myself lying on the hospital bed after a heart attack. I kept thinking to myself, how did this happen? What was I doing wrong? The doctors couldn't tell me. I felt so stupid! What the hell was I doing to myself that caused this heart attack?

A lot. More specifically, what I wasn't doing, I was not loving myself. That ended!

As I sit on the floor today, I can't help but reflect on the journey that brought me here. My 100-Day Journey to Better Health spiritually, mentally, physically, emotionally, and financially has been a long, challenging road filled with twists and turns that I never expected. I've faced heartbreak, loss, and struggles that pushed me to the edge. Yet, as I sit here, at this moment, I feel a sense of calm and peace surrounding me that I never thought was possible. It's taken me a while to get to this point, but I realize now that the key to healing from life's challenges begins with learning to love myself.

For years, I struggled with low self-esteem and a lack of self-love due to domestic violence, adultery, and lack of spousal support. I constantly tried ways to better myself to escape. I sought love and acceptance from people who could never give it to me, leaving me empty and alone.

It wasn't until I hit rock bottom that I realized the only way to heal from life's challenges was first to love myself.

Learning to love me was challenging, however, my life depended on it, and I knew it. I asked God to take me from my misery. He sent me back to learn to love myself and show others how to do the same. I still work on it daily. I realized I needed to make significant changes in my life.

First, I began changing how I talked to myself and replacing negative self-talk with positive affirmations. Next, I started celebrating my wins, no matter how small, and acknowledging my strengths instead of dwelling on my weaknesses. Finally, I learned to forgive myself for my mistakes and past failures, recognizing they were opportunities for growth and learning.

I learned to hula hoop and loved it! I tried different things, even things my friends and family found strange. I kept going even when I didn't want to (and there were a few of those at first). I changed how I ate and took responsibility for learning about food on my own rather than from advertisers.

I documented the many things I tried and what worked and did for 100 days, and the changes were incredible. I tried new things like massage, injections, stretching, and yoga. I changed how and when I worked. I even put my phone on Do Not Disturb over a year ago so that I decide when I am on call. I had to love myself enough to know my path even when those around me did not support me.

Gradually, I made more and more choices in line with my values and what I truly wanted for my life. I stopped seeking validation from others and started trusting my instincts. I pursued things that brought me joy and made me feel alive, regardless of what others thought or said. I began living life with purpose and conviction.

I learned the value of stretching and moving my body anywhere and anytime my body needed it. I saw how quickly my body responded to consistent love and movement.

As I began to love myself more, I noticed a shift in how I approached life's challenges. In the past, obstacles left me feeling defeated. Now, I see them as opportunities to learn and grow. I no longer allowed setbacks to define me but used them as springboards to propel me forward.

The more time I spent loving myself, the more I had to nurture my desire to serve. I have always had it. But, unfortunately, I had gotten confused and put the mask on others first. People began to notice my changes, and I became inspired to help others love themselves too. This meant getting my coaching certification and working with veterans and busy people to help them find their Journey to Self Love.

The journey to loving myself has not been easy, but it has been worth it. Through the ups and downs, I found strength and resilience within myself that I never knew existed. It's an ongoing journey, but the more I love and care for myself, the more I can heal from life's challenges.

If you're struggling to heal from life's challenges, I urge you to step back and focus on learning to love yourself. It may not happen overnight, but it's a journey worth embarking on. Remember, you deserve to be loved and treated with kindness and compassion, especially by yourself.

I am now Coach Yvette Jones - Swanson, M.A. Wellness Coach for busy professionals who think they don't have time or don't know where to start. I am also celebrating the 9th annual Celebration of Life for women veterans through our organization, 100 Pretty Purses for Female Veterans. While I'm accustomed to being busy, this time is different - it's being busy for me. My health, physically, mentally, and spiritually is at the top of my To-do list.

Loving myself and ensuring that I treat myself with kindness and compassion allows me to serve more and more people daily, especially ME!

Commitment to MYSELF!

Dedicated to MYSELF!

Conscious of MYSELF!

Mindful of MYSELF!

Trusting MYSELF!

Caring for MYSELF!

Loving MYSELF!

Yvette Jones Swanson is a dynamic entrepreneur, mother of 2, wife, philanthropist, and #1 bestselling author in the US and Canada. With a professional background dating back to 2000 in veterans housing, Yvette is a certified wellness coach and life strategist. She has dedicated her life to helping others transform their lives by balancing their physical, mental, emotional, spiritual, and financial health. Over the years, Yvette has become an accomplished author, sharing her wisdom and life-changing principles in her books. Her exceptional skills and perseverance have earned her continued recognition.

Aside from her outstanding entrepreneurial journey, Yvette is a devoted philanthropist, passionate about positively impacting the lives of those around her. She regularly gives back to the community, participates in and organizes several charity events and projects, including the annual 100 Pretty Purses for Female Veterans, Celebration of Life Events.

Despite the many responsibilities and challenges of her health and busy lifestyle, Yvette has worked hard to achieve balance in every area of her life. Her dedication to maintaining this balance has made her a source of inspiration to many.

Yvette firmly believes in the statement, "Life is short, so live it to the fullest.". She lives life on her terms with a renewed sense of purpose and fulfillment. Yvette is an inspiration, proving that it's never too late to reshape your life and pursue your dreams.

yvette@vetmentorsllc.com

https://www.facebook.com/YMJonesSwanson?mibextid =LQQJ4d

https://www.linkedin.com/in/yvette-jones-swanson-130a28165

https://instagram.com/yvettejonesswanson?igshid=OGQ 5ZDc2ODk2ZA==

The Dragon Puzzle: My Open Heart

By Dina Fortune

Everything is connected. From how we treat and see ourselves to how we see others, it's all a puzzle to find and feel more love.

I never thought I could write. I saw myself as a mediocre or troubled writer. I'm more of a painter than a writer. At least, that is the childhood story that I continued to repeat.

Despite believing I could not write, I made a decision that I would write and write about things that matter. I want to speak, share stories about life and art, and make a difference. So, I decided to change my story with and about writing, and then I met my friends Raschell and Mistilei.

I knew I wanted to publish my art when I met an author and podcaster, Raschell Harlingten. It was an instant connection, and magic happened... well, more magic. First, I found inspiration in Rachelle's writing as a scribe in the guidance about the art. Then I met Mistilei, a publisher and writing doula who reminded me that my writing is, for me first, a part of my own puzzle.

Self-love started with a decision to follow through. A decision to be open. A decision to let go of the need to be perfect. A decision to be me as perfectly imperfect. Years ago, I started to see connections between things I did not understand. I was curious. With every decision to listen to

46

my curious inner voice, something magical would happen. I noticed my choices counted and took the time to acknowledge this. I call it a read of circumstances. I connect the dots.

Some self-love is standing naked, looking in the mirror, and seeing my beauty because why would I want to see myself as anything other than a work of art?

Some self-love is writing free-hand and allowing sentences to come out however they want. The words come out misspelled and in the wrong order. I allow the flow. I surrender to the piece of me with much to say about love. She does not give a fuck about grammar or making everything just right. There is an editor for that. Everything comes back to love, the chase of it, the surrender to it, the vulnerability, the fear of it, and the sacrifice. It's in ignoring distractions and choosing not to "people please". Letting go of the old stories. Choosing to brush and floss my teeth. Choosing to spend an hour on myself in the morning. Forgiving myself when I hit snooze and celebrating when I get up and do what I said I would. These are my acts of self-love.

No one told me to do these things. No one else is going to do it for me. I see the toll of not taking the time to honor myself is like an active defiant child who doesn't like to be told what to do. She (that defiant part of me) wants to go into the art room and make a mess.

The defiant child has grown up and has decided to make a difference. Now, she/I/me/we live a joyful life, teach and guide others. Formerly Defiant Dina has embraced structure to share her message. Structure allows her to live life and be free. She now sees her circumstances through a lens of compassion, a higher state of consciousness of love and acceptance. She sees others more clearly and is willing to listen to her heart. She's claimed her power, and she has a new ability to listen more deeply, to feel, sense, and touch the hearts of others.

She/I/me/we chose to love the whole me, the entire dragon puzzle, unconditionally. I see myself as a writer of unconditional love.

My mantra is, "I have what I need. Loving myself is knowing that I am enough. I have everything I need within. I do not need to devalue myself or what I have to offer. I have so much love inside of me, and God is within. I AM loved. Loving myself is honoring my gift of life right now".

I did not believe that I was good at writing. I was reminded that I could change that. I can ask for help. I can choose to see myself as a good writer. l started to connect the dots, and I started writing.

I choose to see myself as a good writer. Years and years of believing I was a shitty writer changed instantly. I notice a reverse of words and letters, creating sentences in a nontraditional way. It's like a jigsaw puzzle sometimes. Now that I know it is just this way, a part of me loves to write. I believe I have a new story to tell, a story about how I learned to love myself. I chose to be my best friend and learned to love how I communicate.

The girl inside me that loves to look for distractions, wants to be heard, wants to scream, dance, and punch can now express love.

So, I write for love.

I am a scribe telling a new story of love. I let go of the old story of a girl told she had a questionable future. Medical issues at birth left self-doubt, interruptions, and judgments. Being weird made life challenging.

I write for love. I AM a scribe telling a new story of love. I am letting go of the old story of the girl that was a victim, clumsy, and didn't think she could do much. I knew I had a lot to say and struggled to say it. Communication has always been a huge part of my life. However, I was bullied for being too loud and taking too long to make my point.

My mother sent me to a tutor at a young age to help write a book about my grandmother. It was interesting, short, sweet, and full of love about a misunderstood grandmother, Honey. The memory of Honey reappeared in my life when I was 20. I fell asleep at the wheel on the way home to visit my mother. My grandmother had been on the other side for seven years by then. When I fell asleep, I uprooted three trees and woke up to both of my (deceased) grandmothers screaming in my inner ear as I was about to go over the ledge.

I woke up from my car accident with a new lease on life. I wanted to live life and be empowered. I would not be bullied anymore. I would stand in my power. I moved to another country to learn about another culture, and a new me emerged.

I came home from Italy quite different. I knew I was not disciplined. I was rebellious and wanted to be in the flow, make a mess, and create, create, create! Plans to make a living were not at the top of my priority list. My mother was very disciplined, which I found overwhelming.

I had to let go of my hang ups around discipline and see discipline from the perspective of self-love.

I could finally see discipline as dedication. I took the time to go inward, meditate and look out for my overall higher self. I am grateful for the inner wisdom, the gift of authenticity, and letting go of the feeling of not being enough. I am thankful for the soul family that has shown me my shadows so that I can see my shadow self.

I came into this life to heal the wounds around communication. This shows in my astrology, gene keys, and the story of my life. I choose to love myself beyond all of my imperfections.

I woke from the car accident with new parts of my consciousness. I knew there was something different about me. I was a stronger version of myself.

The post-wreck version of me started to see my magic even when others didn't. I realized I was more than I thought I was. I was more than simply connecting with MYself. I was inspiring myself, my stronger self. I had self-worth and a bright future. I was awake, and my DNA was activated.

My art began to come through me. That was life-changing. I saw myself as a pioneer. I paint galactic beings, not even realizing it. I channel the energy of famous artists, such as Picasso.

I had no idea what started by crashing into three trees. I was learning to communicate in love. I was learning to see things differently.

I knew I was onto something with my art. I met my soulmate, and my art became a communication source. I now communicate with the language of light. This is about love, goes back to source, and has a higher communication to the journey of art and healing myself.

My self-love has also included writing. I chose to rewrite my story. I learned that there was a way to communicate more lovingly with myself. I know I am enough. I am smart enough. I am supported to read, communicate, collaborate, and let go of imperfections.

I can rearrange my story and choose to write the love in words. I am vulnerable and authentic as an act of self-love. I see the story of empowerment in my story and happily share that it's OK to be weird. I've also learned to embrace my weird, funky, and goddess energy. I ask myself, "What does it feel like to look in the mirror and say I love you?"

I returned to art in 2019 to heal my perception of myself and how I saw others and to heal the pattern of feeling like a victim. The desire to heal me was an act of self-love that bled into everything that I do.

I've learned tools to help me meet my goal of writing, like talking into my device, transcribing, and working with someone who can hear and see my words.

I am so grateful for the tool of writing to share on Self Love. I have overcome my fears, my anxieties and am able to communicate. Because I choose to speak with Love, my words flow easily. It's easy when someone listens with an open heart, especially my own!

It is my puzzle, my puzzle, and I love it!

Dina is a lover of all things galactic, art, energy, fairies, dragon, and magical.

Dina has been healing since she started painting five years ago. Through this process, she discovered her gifts as a channeler of Divine wisdom and an intuitive painter. Dina channels soul language and activation codes using her voice, drumming, movement, and painting. Dina is also tapping into the akashic field and can assist others with a deeper connection with themselves, creativity, perspective shifts, sovereignty, and embodiment.

Dina began her dragon journey in 2019 and discovered her purpose when she learned about the Sophia Dragons. Then, as an artist, she realized she was channeling higher-frequency energies through her paintings.

Dina attended a Celtic dragon reiki and Sekkhem empowerment session, where key codes were activated to assist others with their abilities and unique expression.

Dina connects with her role as a Sophia Dragon activator and channels the codes into art for the activation and ascending planet. In addition, Dina has been co-facilitating dragon ceremonies to build the dragon community and call the dragons home in communion with those human partners.

Dina is also an activation artist, authentically serving her clients and the collective. Every session is personalized and can include intuitive card reading, painted light code, spoken soul language, and shamanic singing and drumming.

Instagram @lightlanguagedina and Souly Dina.

https://www.facebook.com/dziskinfortune

https://linktr.ee/lightlanguagedina

In the Mirror

By Nicole Angai-Galindo

I do. I see you. When I look into the mirror, you are staring back at me. So many times, you gazed at me with vacant eyes. Why? So many times, you scrutinized me with a critical eye. Why? I am me. I am you. We are one and the same.

Yes, finally! Training bra time. I was thirteen. Some of my friends already carried around the chest of an eighteen-year-old. Me? I just wanted to fill out my training bra. Haha. I started growing at thirteen and stopped at fourteen. It was like planting a seedling in the dark and never watering it.

Sprouting slowly. Ever so slowly.

I was a flatliner. Not dead. I was still breathing, of course, but a piece of me was dying inside. My self-esteem. As my inhibitions to wear anything I wanted died along with it. So silly. But is it really? When that movie came out back in 1990, I was teased mercilessly. I still have my moments—the ones where I struggle to walk on the beach and be ok. Not feeling the need to wear a cover-up.

The upside-down mop. A stick with lots and lots of hair. Sigh...

Somehow when Daddykins called me Princess Spaghetti, I beamed. Somehow when "they" commented on my boyish figure, I wished my Daddykins were there to protect me. I never really did fill out. Not even after having my son. Now at 46... Well yeah, that's a different story. I filled out the muffin top pretty well!

54

"Why are your front teeth pushed in like that?" An innocent question from that woman's six-year-old daughter. "I don't know," I replied. "God made me this way." I was in my thirties, and a six-year-old had hurt my feelings. She's got a unibrow, I thought. Yeah, I was having not very nice thoughts. If I can't own that now, well, I certainly couldn't have forgiven myself so that I could love myself today.

And I do. I truly do. I'm not sure what happened or when it happened. I woke up one day and just decided I'm done. Done with the ex-boss that told my co-workers, "Tell Marcos to feed that girl." That Marcos is now my husband, and soon we will celebrate our fifth anniversary.

Wait. I'm lying. Let me digress. I know exactly when I shed that ugly skin. The one covered in the scars from the sticks and stones that did not break my bones but broke my confidence. We had a fight. I thought we were friends until she made it very clear we really never were. I told her my mom taught me to say nothing if I had nothing good to say. Her mom had taught her to speak her truth. Two sides of the same coin? My penny, her penny?

Her argument? I did what I did for recognition. I was kind, considerate, generous, helpful, and generally very likable because I was fake. I had to face some hard truths about myself after that. I was a people pleaser. Sigh. Ok, so now what?

Now nothing. I realized that I felt good about myself when I was good to others and that in itself was my self-love - that I was a giver and not a taker. It's not my problem that I'm easygoing and low maintenance, so therefore I have more time to invest in the people around me. I mean,

I'd just as happily do my own mani and have my boo boo trim the ends of my hair instead of sitting in the salon for four hours. Ain't nothing wrong with that. That's just not my thing.

Maybe that was the problem. Some people just couldn't handle me being me and needed to put me down so they could feel better about themselves. Maybe. So many maybe's.

I'm all over the place, I know. That's one of the things about me. I'm just that way. I've come to accept that I am, and I love it. I can jump back and forth between things and even triple dutch, without losing my footing. To think that I let others tell me that my bipolar mind was horrid, making me a horrible person. That's the thing, though. They will say it, you can't stop that, but you can choose to let those words slide right off of your Teflon shoulders.

Every day I tune out the white noise is another day I grow closer to the voice in my heart. The only voice that matters. The only voice I should be heeding. This voice gets me out of bed each day, telling me to breathe deep and to exhale, long and slow.

It is my survival guide, my protector, and when it speaks, I urge myself to listen.

I am still in these moments. Letting the cadence of my inner voice wash over me, letting the words pass through me. And when my pores are saturated with my purpose, I run with it like my life depends on it. Because when suffering from depression, it really does. I take the good days and make them great. I take the bad days and make them good.

Less than six months ago, something happened that brought life as I knew it to an abrupt end. I threw myself into my writing. I allowed myself to be cocooned within my imagination and my passion for creativity, and when I was ready, I exploded from that shell.

Brilliant, tremendous, worth it. Worth every moment of pain, suffering, joy, and laughter. I'd found who I was always meant to be, but I was actually always there, just hiding. Hiding under the protective armor of my smiles that hid the gritted teeth. A sign that I was trying to hold it all together.

Now my exuberance for life, my gratitude for having found myself is as deep as the slashes of flesh to bone, for the weapons I allowed others to wield over me.

There are still skirmishes, occasionally battles but never a war. The day I stopped going AWOL on myself is the day that I ended the war. The warring of guilt within me. For not being enough. I am more than enough for myself, and I found that in finding myself, I am now enough for others too.

My story is enough to touch the heart of a stranger. To show them that to love yourself is the greatest gift you can give, not just to yourself but to everyone around you, everyone who I hope to impact with these words. Fingers flying across a keyboard, thoughts tumbling out to form sentences and paragraphs. To create an emotional entwining of who you are, who I am, and that we are the same. That when I look in the mirror. I see you. I do.

In the Mirror
By Nicole Angai-Galindo

Now I see myself through the windows to my soul. My eyes awash with pride, with adoration at the image reflecting back to me. And in that reflection, I glimpse you. My brothers, my sisters in flesh, in emotions, in hearts that bleed and sing.

So my two cents may not be yours, or it may. Either way, you've seen, heard, and felt the innermost thoughts and feelings of another. Another human being, who at this very moment knows not the faces, the crinkle at your eyes, the upturn of your lips, nor what is in your heart, but still she bares her soul. She lets it all hang out.

Because she knows now that her measure of self-love has always been in how she has treated others. Her actions an extension of her words, her words an extension of her thoughts. And that by changing her perception of the words of others, who have chosen many different names by which she should be called, she disallowed those words to have any meaning.

Instead, she has established her own dictionary, filled with vocabulary that encourages her self-care. To motivate, inspire, and be called to action from within herself. Thumbing through the pages of her mental journals to remind her of the phrases she has coined for herself.

That I am worthy, I have always been. And, when I don't feel that way, it is by my own hand. My accountability is my credibility, for who can I trust if not myself first? My credibility is my authenticity, for the trustworthiness I give myself in showing the world who I am.

Am I now showing the world who I am? Do I now know who I am? Yes!

Once I found myself and my purpose, I could look in the mirror, not with vacant eyes or ones full of judgment but with ones full of admiration and awe.

Once you find yourself and your purpose, you will look in the mirror, not with vacant eyes or ones full of judgment but with ones full of admiration and awe.

You have always been enough, and so am I.

Nicole Angai-Galindo aka Nic is the founder of the Gifted Bipolar Writer. She writes and makes graphics/banners for social media, primarily LinkedIn. She started this business to help people new to social media, to find their niche quickly and build their network steadily. She is also a #1 best selling author and avid blogger. Her blog, This Thing Called Life: Just Doing Me And Rolling With It is about everything life has thrown her way. The good, the bad and the ugly.

Nicole has made many guest appearances in LinkedIn live shows and YouTube where she advocates for mental illness. She embraces her bipolarness as a gift and attributes her talent and creativity in part due to it. Drawing from Two Minds and Two Hearts. She is currently working on a project with Dr. Constance Leyland called, "50 Inspirational Connections" and will continue to collaborate with like-minded individuals to help level up people who entertain a growth mindset. You can find Nic on LinkedIn. Please check her out and join in her live audio room, every Sunday at 10 EST, where a bit of everything is discussed around the central theme of, "Owning your story and letting it be your inspiration to accomplish great things".

https://www.linkedin.com/in/nicthegbw/

Email: nicthegbw@gmail.com

Blog Link: https://medium.com/@nicoleangaigalindo

My Sweet Struggle

By Christine Jones

Self-love has been a journey. Once I started living according to these three principles of morals, values, and ethics, self-love began to take shape. I allowed myself the grace to make mistakes, learn from them, and try hard not to repeat them so they do not become a problem. Once I started living my life purposefully, focusing on self-care and having God at the helm, I discovered self-love.

Creating a space for gratitude has helped immensely. When I focus on being grateful for things in my life, my mind shifts from being critical to allowing myself grace. This practice, along with mindfulness, sets the stage for inner peace. Inner peace is crucial for self-love. I form a stronger relationship with God and others when I have this. My self-love is sweet and overflowing when I have peace as my foundation.

Self-love is evident in how I carry myself, interact with, and treat others. I am kind, considerate, and tolerant of others' differences, and differences are not a threat to my identity. I forgive my mistakes and use them as an opportunity to learn and grow.

Am I attracting people who possess self-love and compassion for others? I need to reflect on my views of myself and my thoughts related to relationships and how I interact with others. Therefore, I must be conscientious of my aura to keep moving forward and have healthy relationships. To know who you are, look at the people you attract.

My journey with self-love has had many struggles. It has been a love-hate relationship at times. When I was little, my self-love was unstoppable. I went to church, learned about a forgiving God, and enjoyed spending time with my family and friends. I suddenly had significant life events happen, and I became self-conscious and more introverted.

Around the age of nine, things changed for me. I struggled in school and was held back, stating I needed to be tested for a learning disability. My self-love took a hit. At this point, I didn't realize I bestowed other gifts. In addition to this, I gained weight and was shunned by my peers. I also developed vitiligo on my face and developed ichthyosis (a skin disorder). My mom was getting remarried, we were moving, and my world had turned upside down. So many changes occurred, and I sought to find where I belonged in my family and school.

After my mom got remarried, I went from being a Protestant to a Catholic. The two churches were worlds apart. One focused on a loving God, and the other felt more judgemental and focused on people's sins. Confession was challenging because I struggled to find things to confess. I found myself looking at my everyday life and concentrating on what was wrong with me, not through a compassionate God's eyes—further damaging my self-worth.

When I was in middle school, I thought I loved myself. Looking back, my self-love came from other people's validations, compliments about my appearance, and how many people liked me. But unfortunately, my shallow view of myself was superficial and lacked a stable foundation, ready to give way at any moment.

My self-love took a nose dive as my hormones changed and I went through puberty. In addition, we moved when I was in the middle of eighth grade. I felt like a fish out of water. I did not fit in. I was used to living in the country wearing bright-colored tops and tight blue jeans, where you had to lay on the bed to get them on. They were too loose if you could stand up and zip them up. They wore pastel, baggy cotton clothes with different hairstyles on the east coast. I became self-conscious. I needed help understanding what they were saying and the accents on the east coast. They talked faster and used different vocabulary. For instance, I would say pop, and they said soda. It made it even more challenging to assimilate with the other students. I was not accepted into the group. I went from being popular to being an outcast. I cried many nights and longed to move back to Ohio.

When I was in high school, self-love was non-existent. I looked in the mirror and didn't like the person reflected. I was critical of myself and magnified every little flaw, and I still didn't fit in. I wasn't receiving validation from others, and my self-esteem took a hit, as well as my self-love. I focused on being popular and climbing the popularity chain, and I spent more time trying to fit in than developing myself. There had to be something wrong with me if I wasn't receiving the validation I was searching for externally. The more critical I became of myself, the more it turned towards self-loath.

On top of this, I also was in much pain due to endometriosis, adenomyosis, ovarian cysts, and IBS. I had a hard time concentrating in class. My cramps were so bad, and the pain was unmanageable that I couldn't attend mentally even though I was physically in class. Sometimes, I was in so much pain I didn't even realize I was missing school. I spent many nights studying to keep up. By this point, I found how I learned best and was compensating for my learning challenges. It was hard to memorize and retain facts, but I could work around this by recording and listening to them while I would say them aloud with the tape recorder.

During high school, I started therapy. I paid for my therapy sessions due to my therapist's suggestion to help take responsibility for my journey. As a teenager, putting my hard-earned money into therapy sessions was costly. I started creating boundaries at home, becoming more aware of my internal self-talk, and doing some inner work on myself. I worked on being more independent. My therapist asked me to write down qualities I liked about myself. I was hard-pressed to write anything down. I could freely write about what I didn't like, but I had a challenging time considering replacing my negative self-talk with something positive.

I chose a college in the Midwest. I found happiness for the first time in a long time. I became a person I was proud of. I was doing charity work and actively involved in my sorority. I was recognized for my good grades.

I got married shortly after college. I was still focused on accomplishments rather than looking internally for my self-worth. I was busy caring for everyone else and neglected to nurture and care for myself. I didn't know who I was or my larger life purpose.

I was a teacher, a wife, and a mom, but who was I as a person? As my marriage deteriorated, so did my self-worth. I was at a shallow period in my life.

My family dynamics were changing, and my family was in turmoil. I could feel my world closing in on me. I was experiencing excruciating period pains and struggling physically and mentally.

As my marriage crumbled, I had a choice of which path I would go down—one of self-hate or self-love. **I chose self-love**. I pulled myself up by my bootstraps and decided I would be a person who was strong, kind, and loving. Once I started to look at my character and focus on character traits, I saw significant positive transformations. I evolved from external to internal validations. As a result, my self-confidence grew, and true self-love started to develop.

I challenged myself to tackle things out of my comfort zone. I needed to make extra money to keep the home for my children. I didn't want to trade time for money. So I decided to open my house for a bed and breakfast to bring in more money for my family. To help get things ready, I learned how to do most of the work myself. I was proud when I learned how to lay a floor. I stuck to it and realized that I had resiliency and was challenging. This momentum built upon itself. In two and a half weeks, I pulled up carpeting, figured out how to texture walls, repainted my home, and learned to ride a lawnmower on treacherous terrain. I tore down a wall and figured out how to finish it later. I also reached out to friends, family and started going to church.

My turning point was when I started to look at grit and perseverance. I was rising above my situation and becoming a person I admire. I was becoming comfortable with the uncomfortable and pushing myself to move out of my comfort zone to accelerate my growth.

Once I realized I could use past or current pain to improve my life and the lives of others. I like to think of it as a bow and arrow. The farther back the bow is pulled, the farther the arrow will go. So in challenging situations, I practice gratitude and mindfulness and figure out how to use this period to create an opposite reaction to keep moving forward.

Self-love has been a journey. I make sure I am very aware of my thoughts because my thoughts are who I tell myself to be. I do not live in isolation; I impact those around me; what we feel inside spills over to how we treat others and talk. We must continually strive for self-love to show up for ourselves and others and be proud of the person we have become. Self-love is a journey of compassion, grace, perseverance, peace, and joy. I look in the mirror and am proud of the person looking back at me. When I struggle, the gift of self-love is all the sweeter.

After 30-plus years of being an outstanding educator, Christine Lynn Jones has embarked on a new chapter in her career, focusing on coaching, public speaking, and delivering inspiring keynote addresses. She aims to positively impact worldwide by leveraging her vast knowledge of educational methodologies and strategies. Armed with a deep understanding of educational best practices and a natural flair for communication, she guides educators toward excellence by sharing practical strategies and fostering a growth mindset. Christine equips fellow educators with the tools and inspiration to create engaging and inclusive learning environments. She champions initiatives that promote innovation, inclusivity, and educational equity, advocating for policies and practices that empower teachers and prioritize holistic student development. Her unwavering commitment to inspiring and empowering educators drives positive transformations worldwide in classrooms, schools, and educational systems. Audiences expect to be inspired, motivated, and equipped with practical tools to enhance their teaching practices.

https://masterconnecter.vip/connect-with-best

www.linkedin.com/in/ christine-jones-cj

https://www.brilliantbeammedia.com/

https://www.facebook.com/profile.php?id=1000934366 27633

https://www.instagram.com/christine__jones0/

An Unpleasant Journey of Life

By Lee Evans

As I sit to write about my two cents on self-love for the third time, I have come to a huge realization, I am still determining what SELF-LOVE is.

I grew up in a broken home in the 1960s and '70s in Arkansas. Divorce was not a common thing. My mother was a stripper and liked to sleep around, so, of course, my dad did not want to stick around. He left us to find greener pastures.

My mother would lock my sister and me in an apartment when I was 3 and 4 years old for days at a time. She would leave a pot pie in the oven for me to eat and two milk bottles in the refrigerator for my sister. I remember waiting for daylight in the windows and would wander around the apartment looking for bugs to eat. The hunger pangs would rack my small body after the pot pie was gone the second day. I did my best to keep my sister fed, giving her a bottle when she would cry. She was two and kept inside the baby crib, where she couldn't get out and wander around.

I don't know where my mother would go. She was apparently a very busy woman. Sometimes she would come home with some drunk man and say he was our new daddy, but that never lasted. Within a few days, she would be gone again, and the familiar apartment would be empty except for the pot pie and two bottles of milk.

An Unpleasant Journey of Life
By Lee Evans

The sun would make its way across the windows, and then darkness would mark the end of another day, and I would crawl into my sister's crib and fall asleep, waiting for the light to come back so that I could hunt for more food. I crawled around in the cabinets and drawers until she returned and brought food, milk, and another man.

Twice my mother placed us in an orphanage. The first time was in Kansas City. I guess she figured that if she took us up there, my grandparents or father could not find us. I was too young to know how long I was there. I only remember being bullied by the older kids. We had very little to eat at meal times, and the older kids would steal what little they gave us. So hunger was an issue again. The next place she took us to was in Oklahoma City. It was smaller but still had kids that bullied for food. I remember that place a little more vividly. It was a green two-story house that had been converted into an orphanage. There was wire mesh on all the windows to keep anyone from being able to climb out and bars on the doors. There was a ten-foot-high fence around the place so no one could leave the yard. The ladies running the place were very cold and seemed to have no feelings for the kids. It was just a job to them. Hard, crunchy macaroni was what they fed us for snacks when we would complain about being hungry. My Grandmother and two aunts found us in both places and brought us back to Arkansas. Eventually, my mother would promise to do better, and they would let her have us back. She would take us right back to that little apartment and leave us.

One day my grandmother found us alone in the apartment. She broke out the front door window so she could unlock the door, come inside and get us. Later in life,

70

she told me that when she peeled our diapers off of us, a lot of our skin came off with the filthy diapers because they had been on us for so long. Neither of us had been potty trained.

She took us home, bathed us, and kept us for nearly two years. She was busy trying to survive with my grandfather, and taking on two non-potty trained children was rough for her. She did her best with us, and I almost started to feel secure after a year or so.

After my fifth birthday, my other grandparents came and took us to see my dad in Tennessee. Little did I know that we were basically being kidnapped and left with my father. He had remarried a wonderful, beautiful lady from Tennessee. It took me several years, but I came to think of her as my MOM. That lady cared for us for seven years as if we were her very own children. I was starting to get comfortable when the rug was pulled out again.

My dad was a truck driver and was gone much more than he was home. I have no idea why, but he had an affair on Mom. She found out, and of course, another divorce ensued. We wanted to live with Mom but were not allowed to because she was only a stepmother. My dad moved us in with his new wife and her two kids. She did not like my sister and me and made sure that she made our life hell when my dad was not there, which was most of the time.

The gory details of that awful year with her made me realize I had to get out somehow. I made plans with my sister to run away and try to get back to Arkansas to be with our grandparents again. Before we could break free, my dad and his wife put my sister in a halfway home for kids who couldn't be controlled. I had no way of contacting or

71

even finding her. Finally, I had enough, and I took off to some friend's house and asked them to contact my grandparents in Arkansas. They did, and the following day I was on a flight by myself to Little Rock.

My grandparents did their best to give me a good home, and we moved to Henryetta, Oklahoma, to run three motels for my Aunt. There I was able to attend my freshman year of junior high and go into high school. I wanted to play sports, and they indulged me. For almost two and a half years we were there, I learned how to make friends. I learned the value of working hard to earn money. I bought myself a motorcycle. That bike was freedom to hold a job at Sonic and make decent money for a teenager. I worked 35 hours a week at Sonic. I have no idea how many hours a week I put into changing sheets, cleaning bathrooms, and making beds at the motels. I also attended school and played sports. For the first time in my life, I truly felt like I belonged somewhere. I grew in self-confidence. My life was good for that short time, and it felt like I had finally realized I had value to people. I mattered.

That all came to a halt in 1979. After two and a half years, my aunt decided to sell the motels, and my grandparents were tired. They wanted to move back to Arkansas to their home. I tried to stay in Henryetta, but at 16, I lacked the skills and discipline to make it on my own. I was soon in trouble and had to return to Arkansas to live with my grandparents. My dreams of getting into college on a scholarship went out the window. The little school I attended in Arkansas had 300 students from 7th grade to 12th grade. They only had basketball as a sport. I hated basketball because I sucked at it. I became restless and bored really fast living in that small town. I turned to using Marijuana and alcohol for recreation.

At 17, I joined the military. The week before I left for basic training, I got my girlfriend pregnant. I learned about it in basic training. I turned 18 while I was at Fort Benning. I was supposed to go through my basic training, then return and finish my senior year of high school. That did not happen. I dropped out of school and took a job at a lumber yard until the military came knocking. They made me get my GED and move on with training. I eventually realized I did not like the Army, and I visited an Air Force recruiter and got myself transferred.

I married my girlfriend after Army Basic and had four beautiful daughters with her. I had never been truly taught the meaning of love. People tolerated me because they had to. That is basically how I dealt with my family for many years. I tolerated them. I loved them in my own way, worked hard and provided for them, and was determined that they would NEVER have to go through what I did while they grew up. But I think the meaning of true love was never inside me up to this point.

In 2012, after 31 years of an okay marriage, we divorced. It wasn't her fault. I just felt like I was not finding what I was looking for. I didn't realize at that time that what I was looking for was love and self-respect. I did not know that too love someone else, and have them return that love, I had to love and respect myself first. At that time, this wasn't something I was capable of.

My second wife could see this about me. She started teaching me that I needed to take care of myself before I could take care of her. She very patiently taught me that I matter, not only to her, but to myself, to my kids, and the world to some extent. She would say, "How do you ever expect to love me if you can't even love yourself?" She would take me shopping and invite me to pick out the clothes I wore instead of just wearing whatever someone bought or gave me. She invited me to pick destinations I wanted to go to and the food we would eat. For the first time in my life, I chose to do things I truly liked or enjoyed doing. In doing this, I came to understand what true love meant. I fell so deeply in love with this woman. She understood that I had no self-worth, and to love her, I had to discover and love myself.

She passed in 2020, and I felt like my world had collapsed. I felt as if I could never take another breath. How would I survive? She was my world. I thought about taking my own life so I could join her. For so many days, I felt like I could not get out of bed and even start another day. Just knowing she was not there to love me and encourage me was the hardest thing in this world I have ever endured. My life as I knew it for those eight years, as wonderful as it had been, was over.

I am now three years on and 59 years old. That pain never went away, but I found that life didn't stop just because I did. There are wonderful people out there that are on a discovery and journey to find themselves after they have lived through tragedy or substance abuse, or even suicide attempts. They didn't know how to love themselves at some point, either. For whatever reasons, they needed to find self-love within themselves so they could move on and live life, not just exist.

I found some of these people recently and have collaborated with them on a book similar to this called "Now What?". I realized I was not alone when reading other authors' stories. There are many people out there who are just like me, hurting or no sense of self-worth. They overcame this by self-realization or finding others to nurture and teach them as my wife did for me. Life did not stop, thank goodness, it just became different.

Do I know what self-love is? If it is understanding that it doesn't matter if you see me as fat, old, or unattractive, I am okay with that. For that alone, I may understand self-love. After all, a very beautiful, incredible lady fell in love with this old, fat ugly guy, and she taught him to understand himself first so that he could LOVE and understand her. There are many good stories in Now What?, which were inspiring and reminded me of what my wife taught me through her patience and love.

My life became different when she passed, and I was alone again. I am genuinely okay with that now. My life has meaning to me. I have wants, likes, and needs that I can fulfill on my own and care for that person looking back at me in the mirror. He may not be the best-looking guy in the world, but he matters!

I matter to the world, and most of all, I matter to myself! I love myself, and I take care of myself first! As my beautiful wife did for me, I invite you to choose self-love. Choose to find a pleasant journey. I did!

An Unpleasant Journey of Life
By Lee Evans

Lee Evans is an Air Force veteran and a 20-year oil field geologist, among many other careers.

Today he is an author, enjoying his retirement and lives his adventures in Western Arkansas, proudly featuring his children and grandchildren.

DRAGON'S GOLD

By Steve Hudgins

The silence is deafening, and the light flickers in a deep cavern. I am a knight, wearing tarnished and banged armor with a hunger and thirst for dragon's gold. The quest is daunting, with battles behind me and yet to come. The gold is always hidden in the deep, dark caverns and often guarded by a hungry and restless dragon.

The breath of the dragon stank and the stench made my soul cringe. Fear permeates from his fiery breath. The all-consuming fire burns souls but never destroys them. His grizzly claws threatened to be hurtful, and the gold seemed outside of my grasp.

College brought the allure of a quest and thirst for knowledge. I might find gold while sinking myself into the depths of academia. The stench of that dragon had stained my soul and seemed to chase my achievements but with no discovery of gold in sight. When earning my shield of a bachelor's degree, armed with my sword of truth, I set out again to look for something that would quench my thirst but was met with opposition from others seeking my gold.

After losing a job due to my insecurities, I thought I would be a failure. Then, I heard a song carried on the wind, and my soul awakened to the music of people singing in cadence. A group of people in battle dress uniforms marched into a seabed of green. I was in the Army now. Could we battle the dragon? Could we find the gold? I found glimpses of gold there. One such quest was a damsel in distress. No other man would step into an honor worthy of their calling. She was pregnant by another man and shunned by her family. I could not let her experience the shame, so I stepped up to the honorable calling and convinced others to join. If I could not help, I used my knighthood, and others protected her when I was called away in battle. We achieved self-sufficiency, and she became a great comrade in arms and friend. While serving, the dragon found me yet again.

This time I felt the scrape of his claw piercing into my flesh, leaving me wounded. The scorching flames left me in the anguish of worthlessness as I once again struggled to reach the gold. When would I encounter the gold? The dragon lurked in the shadows. It was time to pursue this dragon and kill it before it killed me.

I searched for meaning along the journey but could not find it. Marriage was the cure for the quest, or so I thought. There were glimpses of gold with two wonderful children. Yet, the dragon slayed my marriage and devoured my material wealth. Defeated, I sat with burnt armor, scars, and battle wounds. The dragon only got stronger. How would I slay this dragon when I could not glimpse his presence? Just shadows. Or did I?

The dragon left me questioning my self-worth as I realized the dragon had been present since childhood. Recollections play in my memory of constant fighting between my parents and a mother who loved me but not in the way I needed as a child. The phrases "if only you would have listened" and "kids are to be seen and not heard" were seared into my heart like the burning of a fire-breathing dragon. Their transactional love proved that there were no allowances for learning to love me. Failure was not allowed.

The dragon grew and protected the gold treasure even more fiercely with age, yet I was determined to find the dragon's gold. The gold held secrets to many things I searched for, but I lost it in the quest. As the loss of family members and the separation from my children grew, I knew I had to fight back. I wielded my sword once again as custody laws were changed, and I valiantly fought for precious time and won. The battles gave me the courage to exercise my voice, or did they?

I floundered my way around life. What if the quest was not about the search and killing of the dragon for the gold? What if the discovery along the journey needed to teach me something I did not possess?

I nearly lost my life in 2022 as I reencountered the dragon. Mortality faced me, and my mother, the queen, sent only a text to see if I was okay but denied that I even shared what nearly killed me. After a few days, she stopped texting and never called, and I lost track of time while I descended into survival. I needed the gold to survive. One day a queen's letter reached my doorstep, and I hoped it would be a note of encouragement, but it only brought tarnished and scathed words. The mighty sword of her pen crushed my soul with the same sharp tongue as in childhood. I asked to visit them because my father had fallen ill, but I was denied. She wrote, "A self-willed child who is stubborn and rebellious to authority will always find blame." In my mind, I thought, "Really?" When you were bigger than me in my childhood and, in the name of love, sat on top of me or switched me in the discipline of love? It marked me with doubts about loving myself. Yet, the letter continued, "You have love and were shown love, but it does not fit into your narrative that you built your whole life around...to you, it is all about being a victim (narcissism)." I thanked God I mustered the strength never to treat my children with such contempt. While she may have thought those actions were loving, they set me up for this battle within.

The dragon finally showed itself. I was shocked that I did not see the dragon shadow lurking around me. However, in self-discovery, the dragon was me! It took work to dig into my heart with a therapist, and then I became a therapist to see me, the dragon. The gold my dragon guarded was my self-love. I allowed the past to be poisoned. With every quest, I drank the poison that turned me into a hideous beast. Finally, I learned not to kill the dragon but made peace with the dragon. The gold appeared during the pursuit within my soul because it was hidden within the dragon.

The dragon's gold required that I learn to love myself. Self-love is not found outside of me, for I discovered that God within me provided the needed love and acceptance. It did not matter about the trauma or the inflicted wounds from others that pained me. I tamed the dragon that tried to define me.

I renewed my faith, was baptized in water, and was utterly immersed in my new heart. Through the love of God, I had to learn that unconditional love was found in the water, which provided me with a clean conscience and doused the flames of the dragon within. I found my identity and tried to make amends with my mother, but she denied my request and blocked me. I learned that boundaries protect the gold of self-love. I forgave myself for not being at peace, which helped reveal the golden treasure. I learned not to allow people to assign their perceived value to me, as only I would ultimately determine my self-worth and value.

Today, stop me and ask me, and I will show you. I carry a napkin, notebook paper, and a dollar bill as a reminder of self-love and my value. It is more than two cents. It is priceless. A napkin is to wipe up things and yet can be assigned the value of two cents. A notebook paper can be worth a nickel, but it is worth more if I wrote an "IOU" of $100.00. A dollar is a dollar. I have learned that in the past, others have assigned their value to me, and I performed how they expected.

Please, do not believe I am the napkin to clean up the messes. I am not the notepaper for others to write all over me. I am not the $1.00 that feels spent or used. Instead, I learned to be the tree that stands strong and carries self-confidence in knowing the value of the tree's spirit and that I am priceless.

What if self-love does not come with two cents of valuing an opinion but becomes priceless when I respect my boundaries? Self-love is not based on the value of others but on how I view myself as a priceless treasure. Not in a boasting way, but in a confident way of knowing I belong to the Creator, and my value is priceless. Self-love is knowing whose I am, who I am, and what I will be!

Therefore, I learned not to allow anyone to determine the value of my self-worth. It only causes bitterness and confinement, as you have read. Knowing my worth allows me to know my freedom of how to spend my confidence. Spend it wisely and teach the dragon to protect the gold of self-love.

As a two-time international best-selling author, Steve Hudgins, LPC-S, NCC, continues to write to help others to become a better you. His past experiences have created the wisdom of a highly effective therapist. He continues therapy to help couples and men to thrive in their marriages. He is currently licensed as a professional counselor in Oklahoma and Texas. Steve is working on his educational doctoral degree in Community Care Counseling, emphasizing family and marriage, from Liberty University. In addition, Steve hosts a podcast called Coached Soul to help listeners to become "a better you." His battles have made him a therapist who can sympathize and empathize with a proper understanding of what others are going through. His future is bright with the potential of more books, an opportunity as a professor at a local university, expanding his podcast, and supervision of future therapists.

You may contact him at:

www.prcounseling.com

www.coachedsoul.com

steve@prcounseling.com

The Illusions of Comfort: A Soul's Journey

By Julia Caton

Note: This is a sequel to my previous chapter at the beginning of this book.

This morning I saw an approaching storm; the clouds exuded their energy and power. I felt it all around me. I could hear the rooster in the barn next door crowing to let us know he and his hens were ready to be let out- to explore their day with pure abandonment. I let them out, then quickly entered the main house to boil some water for my morning dose of nutrition and make fresh eggs just gathered. I found myself mesmerized by the storm as I viewed it from the kitchen window. The field outside glistened as the rain began to pour harder and faster.

My cabin was nearby, but getting there would require an umbrella. I grabbed one by the door, and stepped outside into the downpour. Then as instantly as I had opened my umbrella to protect me from the shock of the cold drops and sting of their landing on my skin, I closed the umbrella and allowed myself to feel every drop on my face, head, and arms. It hurt, and then it felt alive... The rain was breathing into me, speaking to me.

I was embraced by the soaked tenderness of the grass under my bare feet. I felt the energy all around me! It was a call to blend with the storm, to play with it like a wild child full of vitality, wonder, and vibrance, like a wild animal, viral, powerful, and dangerous! For a moment, as I breathed in the electrifying sensations coursing through my being, I realized the storm didn't just invite me, I had become the storm. The words of a recent quote I heard-from the *I Am Discourses* were felt and heard deep in my chest, **"I am here, and I am there"**; I am a part of everything, and everything is a part of me.

At the time I am writing this chapter, I am about four weeks from the moment where I had laid down on the floor of my cabin in a storm of emotions. I was hurting with unimaginable pain from the detox processes of life, medications, foods, memories, ideas, beliefs, emotional entrenchments and entanglements, societal toxins, conditionings, and a fuck ton of co-dependency.

That twenty-four-hour period on May 15, 2023, was the moment I realized my crucible was every bit of all I clung to for nearly 52 years. It was as though I were walking to my own crucifixion, carrying my cross upon my back. I had to name every splinter of wood digging into my soul. Every tear I shed was like blood flowing from my being demanding to be let go, and every emotion claimed its space as though it had a right to burden my steps under its weight.

That night, I went to my own death, fighting the only monsters that exist; the ones I created from birth to justify, help versions of me survive and give me a false sense of control over what was never mine to control and carry. They had all accumulated into the messy, self-harming version of my personal crucible. From light to darkness, I finally fell asleep, having faced every aspect of myself, then sacrificed it all for the unknown, even at the risk of mortal death that night. There was no more running, excuses, or entertainment for the existence of playing small. I closed my eyes, and in sleep *that* Julia died.

On May 16ᵗʰ, 2023, I was resurrected. A new Julia had risen from that grave on the cabin floor. In every sense of the imagination, I met God during that last twenty-four hours. I am not speaking of religious beliefs or ideations; I am referring to God within. I am talking about God outside of me. I am speaking of the recognition; I am God, and God is me. There is no separation.

I knew instantly who this soul being was and is, how exquisitely I was loved, how much creative powers were within me, how every single experience I had in this mortal body was, in fact, of my soul's making an agreement to experience and learn. I was unequivocally responsible for every single moment of each encounter with life. The expression and tangibility of clarity - there is no right or wrong, no good or bad, no positive or negative, no birth or death in the sense I had previously thought. There was only contrast and transition. Contrast and transition are the necessary key elements of growth, and my soul required immense and extraordinary experiences with both to get me to May 16ᵗʰ!

I had to come to my own death, all my own *Illusions of Comfort* I previously held onto. For those not yet understanding, take a look at what you cling to − If you have to defend it, protect it, feel offended by it, judge it, feel you need to interject yourself into it, think you cannot live without it, have placed your power in it, sacrificed your energy, emotions or resources to it, think you can't do it, say you love it, find yourself unable to control it, have no sense of when you do it or think you will never grow past it, were taught or conditioned to believe it, those my friend, are all your *Illusions of Comfort* – They are YOUR addictions, YOUR lies and they are holding YOU back from everything that is right outside of them all.

At some point in the history of your soul's journey, you will have to choose if you are okay with walking in the calm rain and living this life with whatever shows up. You may choose to walk under shelter into a raging storm, thinking some thin mechanism or tool will keep you safe. However, for some of you, like me and so many others before me, you will walk into that storm as though it is your very breath, and in fact, it will be. You will no longer be walking in the storm, you will have become it. Your *Illusions of Comfort* will have gone their way of death, and you will have risen into a new being of understanding, strength, freedom, and joy. You will come to the place of comprehension, **"I am here, and I am there."** You will have met God- and in so doing, finally come home to yourself.

I bless you with the most beautiful and brutal experiences- may the contrasts and transitions feed your soul's call. Feel it all. Hold a space for each moment of interaction. Be purely intimate, present, and vulnerable. You are everything, and everything is you. This is the ultimate core expression, in my experience, of self-love.

In Pure Bliss, Love, and Light,

Julia Caton, the 918Coach

The Illusions of Comfort: A Soul's Journey
By Julia Caton

Julia, a two-time international and three-time US, and Canada bestselling author, has spent the last ten years focusing on mental health, well-being, and spiritual and ministerial guidance. Julia has an undergraduate degree in Human Development and a graduate degree in Human Relations focusing on Clinical Mental Health. Julia has numerous coaching specialty certifications, and a successful therapeutic coaching ministry. Currently, Julia is exploring writing and publishing opportunities with Campgroundtbd Publishing. Julia is the smiling co-host with the feminine perspective on the podcast, The Coached Soul, with Steve Hudgins. Julia is the content creator and collaborator for the *Illusions of Comfort,* as she exemplifies the values found between Contrast and Transitioning.

Your mental health matters. Your soul's call matters. If you are looking for a methodology process with a whole being perspective on healing, reach out to 918CoachJulia.

TicTok @juliaicaton

918coach.com

LinkedIn www.linkedin.com/in/juliacaton

Green Lights and Parking Spaces

By Deborah Driggs

Having written over one hundred blog posts and having a specific category called "Self-Care," I definitely have formulated my two cents in my writing. In all honesty, my favorite topic to write about is self-love. In reflecting back on my life experiences and challenges, I discovered a common theme in my life: a lack of self-love, self-esteem, and self-care. If the most powerful thing you can do in life is love yourself, and I believe it is, then I wanted to understand on a deep level just what that meant.

Self-love is a crucial aspect of our mental health and emotional well-being. It is the act of treating yourself with kindness, compassion, and respect. It is a practice. Hear me now when I say, "There is nothing to be fixed!" No magic pill, vacation, relationship, new car, fancy drink, or money will "fix" anything. Those are what I call five-minute fixes. The dopamine from those external fixes last five minutes—that's it. You are better off getting a dog: at least you'd have ongoing dopamine hits.

Self-love is acknowledging and accepting yourself for who you are, including your strengths and weaknesses. We are all unique; even identical twins are unique. We are all extraordinary and special in our own way. Comparing ourselves to others is usually where the struggle and negative self-talk starts. By the way, even jokingly saying "I am so stupid" or "I am depressed" tells the cells in our body and sends our brain a message that we are stupid and depressed. Even if it is a joke, it is harmful. On some deeper level, we believe that joke. Whenever I hear people laugh and say, "I am such an idiot," I think to myself, "Wow, they believe that on some level."

The way in which we speak about ourselves, even in jest, can be damaging. Our language is so important. Today I am constantly saying, "Cancel, cancel, cancel!" when I catch myself putting out something that will not serve me. Even if I think I am being funny, that is usually just a way to completely disconnect. People will laugh or smile when they are nervous or filled with fear. They will make fun of themselves and say it's just a joke, but really it is a lack of self-esteem.

Here are some phrases to remove from your speech and thoughts right away: "I'm always," "I never," "I'm trying," and anything derogatory about yourself. Even if you are joking, remove it now. This is where the practice begins. The next time you catch yourself using one of these phrases, say "Cancel"—for example, "I'm always late," "I am always tired," "I never get my way," "I'm trying to feel better." I'm sure you can think of other examples. Just removing this sort of language is a very good start.

The cells in the brain *love* gratitude! Everything and everyone loves gratitude. But we are speaking of self-love, and my two cents is that the cells in your brain and your body absorb what you say to yourself and what you say out loud. Imagine having a brand-new computer or device in front of you and not knowing how to use it. I can tell you there are hundreds of features on my computer I am not accessing. The same is true of our personal system. How we use it is everything!

I like to reboot my computer, turn it off once in a while, treat it well with kindness and gratitude, be happy when it works properly, shut it off at night, and leave it alone for twenty-four hours if it acts wonky. I treat myself this way today. I program myself every morning. I have rituals and practices that guide my day. (In a blog post entitled "Creating Rituals," I give several examples and ideas of what my day looks like.)

I start out by simply saying, "Thank you, thank you, thank you!" I look at myself in the mirror and say, "Wow, look at your sixty-year-young, experienced body. I put my hands on my belly because I think that is the emotional home of our bodies, and I say, "Thank you. I send you so much love!" I care for this body in a profound way. It has served me well and healed quickly anytime I have been sick, so I remember that and fill my mind with so much gratitude and tell the cells in my body, "Thank you for being so strong and never taking a day off to serve me. I also thank my lungs, which breathe without my having to do anything. I'll admit, sometimes I forget to breathe, so I give myself some nice deep breaths. Our bodies are miracles!

When you love your body, and you tell it so, you shift your language and become aware of what you say and put into the universe. You practice self-care. This is a priority. This includes taking care of your physical health by getting enough sleep, eating a balanced diet or what the body is craving, and exercising regularly. It involves taking care of our mental and emotional health by engaging in activities that bring us joy and relaxation, such as reading, practicing yoga, being in nature, cooking, and meditating. Self-care is not a luxury; it is a priority. When was the last time you soaked in an Epsom salt bath? Or dry brushed your body followed by a cold shower? Practice does not make perfect; it makes better practice. This is why I love yoga. There is no destination. It is an ongoing practice. You are where you are in the moment.

I can share from experience I never did any of this until I got into my forties. I had what I call a glimpse here and there of this way of living, but it wasn't until I hit forty that I began a journey. That journey led me to where I am today. We are never too old to start. I am going to be sixty this year, and I feel as though life finally makes sense. I am not swimming against the current anymore, and if I start to do that, I remember that working so hard will not serve me. My journey did not start off with green lights; it included a lot of red lights and fighting against everything and everyone. It was darkness and emotional sadness where I thought at times I was losing my mind. I wasn't ready for the practices I do today, but I was headed there, and it takes what it takes. For me, it took a life event that created instability and major fear—toppled by an addiction. Let's just say I did not see my green lights and parking spaces—you know, when you pull into a parking lot, and magically you get a great spot!

Self-love is a decision to not accept anything or anyone who doesn't serve your highest good or make you a better person! By the way, a lot of people wear great disguises and will make you feel as though they have your back. This I know for sure: the more work you do on yourself, the clearer this gets when you meet people or look around at the people who are in your life. Your perspective will shift, and those people you allowed in at one time will lose it when you let them go. They will begin telling you how horrible of a person you are, or they will ask, "Why are you blowing me off?" You see, when you change and go on a self-love journey, it is hard to bring along people who are self-destructing.

This brings me to boundaries. Self-love is also setting healthy boundaries and saying no when necessary. The people you might be leaving behind will absolutely not like being told no. I have received scathing texts from those I have had to let go—those who made *my* journey about them and their feelings. As people on a self-love journey, we would never send those kinds of texts or guilt trip anyone in our lives. We just let things be. That is love—to love under any condition. When we begin a journey of healing and self-love, it is what is *best* for our mental and emotional life. The universe will show us who is about love and who is about ego. That becomes *very* clear. Make no mistake: you will find out who is about love very quickly.

I believe that disasters can become great masters. I spent a lot of time on the disaster side of things. So I send those people a lot of love, and they remain in my prayers. However, I do not need to engage in anything ever again that does not bring love and joy. It is that simple. Boundaries allow us to prioritize our own needs and communicate our limits to others effectively. This is not about proving anything. Once you give a *no*, that is the end of the conversation. I have said no and gotten back different responses, such as "I feel like you're ignoring me" and "You never call me. Did I do something wrong?"

Boundaries can be the hardest part of this practice because you will get responses that do not serve you and might make you feel bad until you realize they have zero to do with you. You find out quickly who does not like being told no!

Since I have gone within on my journey, I have lost family members and so-called friends. It happens when you begin to choose your emotional health over anything else. I send them *all* love and forgiveness and remember everyone is on a different journey. I stay close to those who do not make me feel bad about myself. That may sound easy, but in my life experience, it is the absolute hardest thing to do. So congratulations if you are on a self-healing, self-love, and self-compassion journey.

This whole self-love idea is not about thinking "I am great"; that is ego. Self-love is an essential aspect of our mental and emotional well-being. It involves treating ourselves with kindness, compassion, and respect, acknowledging and accepting ourselves for who we are, and prioritizing our own needs. This guarantees a life that is filled with joy.

Gratitude is always the key practice. I practice gratitude every day by finding surprises and unexpected moments and acknowledging they exist, like green lights and parking spaces. Remember, my reader, that self-love is a practice! If you have the mindset that this is an ongoing practice and there is nothing to fix, you will understand and thrive in this new way of being.

The greatest news of all with self-love—and this is just my two cents: you will never have to seek validation or approval from another human being ever again. You will attract new healthy, authentic, and fulfilling relationships. That is the gift of this work.

That's my two cents!

Deborah Driggs is on a healing path. Known for her acting roles in *Night Rhythms*, *Total Exposure*, and *Neon Bleed*, she has also been a *Playboy* centerfold and cover girl, a member of the Screen Actors Guild, and a top-rated insurance industry professional. Deborah has overcome a number of challenges by being willing to take risks and maintain a positive attitude. Pursuing her interest in dance, Deborah won a spot on the US Football League cheerleading squad and joined a professional dance company touring Japan. When she returned to Los Angeles, she began her modeling career and auditioned for *Playboy*. After posing as a centerfold, she was invited to grace the cover of the March and April 1990 issues of

Playboy—the leading men's magazine in the world at the time—which led to opportunities as a VJ (video jockey) for the Playboy Channel's *Hot Rocks* show and appearances in several rock videos. Dedicated to helping women break through negative self-talk and take on any challenge, Deborah knows the difference it can make to have a helping hand when one needs it the most. Her response to internal struggles is, "If there is a struggle, then there is a problem, and in that problem, there is a beautiful, simple solution for complicated souls!"

Her book *Son of a Basque* is out now!

Deborah's self-care blogs are available at
www.DeborahDriggs.com

Road to Redemption

By Darryl Langeness

Every journey begins with a single question. For me, that question was, "Who am I?" This query, simple on the surface but profound in its implications, echoed through the chambers of my soul. As I peered into the mirror, the reflection staring back seemed like a stranger, a composite of the expectations, disappointments, and traumas that had shaped me into the person I was.

One morning, as I was about to embark on a trip from Detroit to Minnesota for my uncle's funeral, this question was more potent than ever. The city was experiencing historic floods, my windshield cracked just 40 miles into the trip, and my spirits sank deeper than the floodwaters themselves. The road that lay before me was a familiar one, a path I had traveled annually during childhood Christmas visits to my father's family.

The journey was always arduous—a dull drive through an unchanging landscape leading to a small farm town where I felt like a misplaced puzzle piece. There were no kids to play with. Waking up early and going to bed early was not something I was accustomed to as a city kid. My cousins lived an hour away and were older than me, so we had nothing in common when they visited.

Lacking commonality was also a familiar feeling. Because I was a tall kid who stood out in the crowd, older bullies frequently targeted me. My discomfort with my height was mirrored in my mother's own struggle with her stature. The story I told myself was that my height made me a victim, a belief that had seeped into the bedrock of my identity so much that I held a deep seeded belief that I did not belong anywhere except on a basketball court.

This trip, however, was different. It was my first time back in Minnesota since my father's funeral four years prior. As I drove through the heartland with the same old thoughts, something shifted as I crossed into Wisconsin. The sunrise painted the world with an ethereal glow, transforming the mundane into the magical. Tears welled in my eyes, not of sadness but of overwhelming beauty.

"Have I been so blind to such beauty?" I wondered. "What else have I been missing?" As these questions circulated, I felt a dam break within me. The narratives I had constructed around my life started to unravel, revealing new perspectives.

This shift in perception was like a thunderbolt, illuminating the landscape of my life in a new light. Past traumas morphed into valuable lessons. The bullying I endured because of my height no longer felt like a curse but a catalyst that made me more resilient. The struggles of having an emotionally unstable, disabled sister who made life hell suddenly shifted to empathy. I realized it gave me the strength to help others who may not be in a position to help themselves. It struck me that it was not the facts of my past that had imprisoned me but the stories I had woven around them.

Arriving at my destination, I first visited my father's grave. I poured my heart out as I sat under the open sky. I shared my revelations, my regrets, and my apologies. I questioned and listened, cried, and laughed. In that sacred space, I felt an unburdening of my soul, a feeling of liberation that I had not experienced in years. Part of me died that day; it was the greatest gift I'd ever given myself.

The rest of the trip was imbued with this newfound energy. I realized that life was not just happening to me but for me. Every event and every encounter was a chance to learn and grow. This perspective shift was not just an intellectual understanding but a profoundly emotional one.

My story, just like yours, is a tapestry woven from a myriad of experiences, emotions, and lessons. It is a tale of transformation from self-doubt to self-love, from resentment to gratitude, from feeling lost to finding purpose.

In my journey, I discovered that the quality of questions I ask myself determines the quality of my life. When I replaced "Why me?" with "What can I learn from this?" I empowered myself. My focus determines my reality, and by shifting my focus from my traumas to my triumphs, I could rewrite my story. We all can.

The power of gratitude is another potent force I discovered on this journey. Gratitude is the lens that colors our world with positivity. By expressing gratitude for our journey, strengths, and weaknesses, we can transform our perspective and relationship with ourselves.

It was during this introspective journey that I learned to truly love myself. Self-love is not just about feeling good or pampering oneself; it is about accepting ourselves and embracing our uniqueness. It is understanding that external circumstances or opinions do not determine our worth.

These exercises helped me in my journey and can assist you in yours. These are not just practices but powerful tools that, when used consistently, can create lasting change.

Mirror Exercise: Every morning, look at yourself in the mirror. Look into your own eyes, take a deep breath, and say, "I love you." You can use your name like I do - "Darryl, I love you." Say it with a smile, with energy, and let your body feel the wave of positivity. This simple act triggers dopamine production, leaving you feeling happier and more motivated.

Accomplishments List: Set a timer for five minutes and write down as many of your accomplishments as you can think of. They don't all have to be major accomplishments. It could be as simple as learning to ride a bike, making a new friend, or finishing a book. Recognizing your achievements helps you realize your capabilities and builds confidence.

Celebrate Yourself: After every accomplishment, no matter how small, celebrate. It could be a self-congratulatory pat on the back, a little dance, or treating yourself to your favorite snack. This practice helps to reinforce positive behavior and makes you feel good about your achievements.

These exercises are simple yet profound. They have the power to shift your perspective, turn self-doubt into self-belief, and cultivate a deep sense of self-love. But remember, the magic lies in consistency. Make these exercises a part of your daily routine and watch the transformation unfold.

In the words of Buddha, "*You, yourself, as much as anybody in the entire universe, deserve your love and affection.*" Love yourself, not despite your flaws and mistakes, but because of them. Because it is these unique features and experiences that make you who you are. And who you are is absolutely remarkable.

As you move forward, bear in mind the lessons learned. Embrace the idea that where focus goes, energy flows. If we put our energy into self-love, positivity, and growth, that's where our lives will head. We are the architects of our reality, the authors of our own stories. We can choose to write a narrative of self-love, acceptance, and growth.

Recall that life happens for us, not to us. Each experience, each encounter, and each challenge we face is an opportunity for growth, a chance to learn and to evolve. Our past traumas are not mere sources of pain; they can also be rich wellsprings of insight and wisdom if we shift our perspective.

Understand that our lives are shaped not by the facts of our experiences but by the stories we weave around them. It is not the events but the meanings we assign to them that determine our reality. By shifting our narrative, by telling a different story, we can transform our lives.

Practice asking better questions. Instead of asking, "Why me?" ask, "What can I learn from this?" Instead of focusing on the problems, focus on the possibilities. By asking better questions, we can find better answers and, thus, create a better life.

And lastly, cultivate the power of gratitude. Gratitude is like a magic wand that can transform the mundane into the magical, the ordinary into the extraordinary. Practicing gratitude can infuse our lives with joy, love, and positivity.

And as you embrace gratitude, consider this: you are an active participant, not just an observer in your life. You're not just on the receiving end of your experiences. You are the co-creator of them. Every thought, every action, and every decision you make shapes your reality. So, harness the power of gratitude, and take ownership of your journey. Use it as a compass to navigate life's ups and downs, uncover the lessons hidden within your experiences, and create a life that truly reflects your authentic self. It's your life, your story. So why not make it a masterpiece filled with joy, love, and positivity?

I invite you to this: In those inevitable moments when doubt, stress, or negative self-talk creep in, I challenge you to hit pause. Take a deliberate, deep breath. Allow yourself to remember and relive three instances in your life for which you feel profound gratitude. No moment is too grand or too trivial. Immerse yourself in the memory, and re-experience the joy, the love, and the sense of accomplishment. Let gratitude fill your spirit, lighting your way forward.

This simple yet powerful act of turning to gratitude can provide the clarity and peace needed to continue on your journey of self-love.

Embarking on the journey of self-love, you'll discover it's not a destination but a continuous exploration of your worth and uniqueness. This journey is your personal story, and there's no race. You hold the pen; you control the pace.

Equipped with an open heart, a brave spirit, and the tools from your toolkit, there's no limit to how far you can go. The question, "Who am I?" invites self-discovery, leading to a deeper, more meaningful relationship with yourself.

As you journey, remember it's about embracing your imperfections, finding strength in vulnerability, and wisdom in experiences. You are extraordinary, deserving of your own love and affection. In this journey, you'll radiate love, causing a ripple effect that can transform the world.

You're not alone on this path; we are all travelers sharing stories and lessons, inspiring and supporting each other. So, love yourself, embrace this journey, and celebrate every step. Each moment is a victory. And as you discover the love you have for yourself and the world, you'll realize that in loving ourselves, we can truly love others, and together, we can change the world.

Darryl Langeness is a Neuroencoder and the founder of Mindset Badass. After decades of negative self-talk and self-sabotage, through pain and perseverance, he overcame and created the life he once only dreamed of. His mission is to guide others, held back by self-doubt, on the same transformative journey.

Darryl's approach ignites inspiration, possibility, hope, and joy within his clients. He helps you reprogram your mind, leaving procrastination, hesitation, and self-doubt behind. Mindset Badass is your ticket to transforming dreams into reality, rediscovering your passion, and embracing the superstar within. Darryl will help you embark on a journey to the re-energized life you were meant to live!

If you have been struggling with an internal battle and negative self-talk that sabotages your visions and dreams, break free and discover the next steps to be your authentic self. Schedule a phone call with Darryl Langeness at www.mindsetbadass.com/contact.

Follow on Facebook or visit www.mindsetbadass.com

Uncovered Strengths

By Tammy Thomas

Self-love is a transformative journey that goes well beyond physical appearance, but in my personal experience, it played a significant role in my weight loss journey. Over ten years, I embarked on a mission to be happy and fell in love with myself. I released 135 pounds for good. This process not only transformed my body but also revolutionized my entire life. The impact of self-love has been profound and everlasting.

When I began my journey, I realized self-love was more than accepting and appreciating my physical appearance. It required me to spend time alone. In my times of complete isolation, I could delve deep within myself and discover who I truly was. I did not allow myself to reach out to toxic friends and family members for support. I did not want anyone to tell me it would be okay or too hard.

For the first time, I was the only one that got to choose what was possible. This self-discovery was a crucial aspect of the process, as it allowed me to understand my values, passions, and purpose in life. By truly knowing myself, I gained the power to set boundaries and prioritize my well-being above all else.

Choosing myself first became a fundamental part of my self-love journey even in challenging situations. In the beginning, I didn't even realize I was putting myself first. When I began to love myself truly, it just came naturally. I learned to listen to my needs and desires and make decisions aligned with my authentic self. This meant saying no to things that didn't serve me, whether unhealthy friendships, toxic environments, or detrimental habits. By prioritizing my well-being, I began elevating my self-worth and refused to settle for anything less than I deserved.

Throughout this transformative process, I experienced the gradual realization that my self-love journey had far-reaching implications. It extended beyond my physical appearance and permeated all aspects of my life. As I fell in love with myself, I started to build the body of my dreams through a combination of drinking Kangen water, eating whole real food, regular activity, and self-care. My self-care included a nightly soak in an Epsom salt bath, grounding in nature, and gardening. I grow herbs and vegetables. I love to have my hands in the dirt. I meditate daily. I source, choose, and prepare whole, nutritious food from scratch with love. A big part of self-care for me is journaling. I have been writing the life of my dreams. #QW300, As I have released the weight, the life of my dreams have changed. The weight I released was a tangible representation of the internal changes I had undergone.

However, self-love didn't stop at the physical transformation. It ignited a chain reaction that led to creating the relationships of my dreams. I was married when my self-love journey began. He joined me on my self-love journey. He also spent plenty of time getting to know and love himself. By loving and respecting myself, I attracted people who treated me with the same level of care and kindness. I inspired some of my friends to believe in themselves. Toxic connections faded away; this was always hard. It almost always hurts. A loss is a loss, even when it makes room for supportive and nurturing relationships that uplift me. I discovered that when I loved myself deeply, I could form connections built on mutual respect and genuine love.

Self-love also allowed me to find my passion for health and pursue it with unwavering determination. I discovered my unique gifts and talents as I became more familiar with who I was. I am an energy healer. I have a unique ability to absorb negative energy and transmute it into positive. The more I accepted my authentic self, the more my passion flourished. I pursued my dreams with a newfound sense of purpose and joy, knowing I was honoring my true self.

One of the most remarkable aspects of self-love is that it is an ongoing process. As I continue to love and accept myself unconditionally, I peel back layers of self-discovery, unveiling incredible strengths and qualities that were previously hidden. Each layer of my journey brings new opportunities for growth and self-acceptance. I am constantly amazed at the depths of my inner strength and resilience.

Falling in love with my reflection has been quite the process. I was not familiar with body dysmorphia; however, it is real. I did not see myself like everyone else did, or so it seemed. I don't think I ever accepted the really fat me. 275 pounds is huge. I refused to be in pictures. I did not seek out mirrors; hell, I refused even to weigh myself. I did not like me. I slowly began to appreciate my reflection as the weight was released. Baby steps, I fell in love with my shadow first. She was so slender and willowy. Was that really my shadow? I got to know her first.

I embarked on a journey of self-acceptance using my shadow. She was slender and willowy. She was feminine and beautiful. She was elusive and cautious. She was creative and confident. She was loyal. She was always with me. She became me, and I became her. I found that the more I became my shadow, the more I fell in love with the reflection of me I see in the eyes of my friends and loved ones.

One powerful symbol of my self-love journey is a picture of my current self. No makeup, my hair is a mess, and it is one hundred percent me. The light shining from my eyes in this picture serves as proof of the joyful state I am abundantly blessed to live in. It is now my screen saver. Every time I look at it, I can't help but smile. It serves as a reminder of how far I've come and the love and care I have invested in myself. Seeing my own reflection with pride and contentment is a testament to the power of self-love.

Self-love is a transformative process that goes beyond physical changes. It is about knowing who you are at your core, setting boundaries, and prioritizing your well-being.

By falling in love with myself, I released excess weight and built a life filled with authentic, supportive relationships as I pursued my passions. Each layer of my self-love journey uncovers new strengths and qualities, leading me to true unconditional love and acceptance.

I Am grateful for the profound impact self-love has had on my life. I am excited to continue growing and embracing my true self. With each layer, I uncover strengths and gifts I never knew or even forgot I had.

Tammy Thomas is a 51-year-old woman who has done and continues to do the work. She has accomplished lasting weight loss. She is happily married to her husband of 18 years. Living a life of joy and acceptance has become her passion as she becomes ready to accept her many healing gifts. The ability to reexplore forgotten or never known gifts is what currently lights her up. She is in the process of opening a health and wellness center in her small town. She will focus on different natural healing methods, whole foods, blissful friendly activities, and lovely high-frequency connections.

My Beast

lay silent, sleeping

until blazen-wild
she-wolf eyes
awakened him

he had tamed his fiery gaze and blood-less canines
now, for centuries

since that time

creating a fearful heart in one
who once loved him,

turn petrified and grey
that missus saw his pure beat

and

never could erase the sweat from his bared teeth
extended claws, ripened for tear

gasps inside a mother's breath

externalized full fight, red screens overtaking
diplomacy, alpha has arrived

nakedly discovered in an open field,
without cover

freshly shaven, maybe fur-less parts, shots fired off,
he scuttered

and
lost, his zest

his breadth for life
passion squandered, splintered, and caged

carry on like nothing happened
for minutes upon hours upon days, this is lacking life

turning inward, where else to hide

the missus doesn't see him, passing by
but he still sees him in her eyes

then one day, he says goodbye, not really realizing exactly
why

drifted apart
is all he knew

too silent now surrounded by daft and deadened air
feeling scratchy, itch-free skin

he crawls into sleeping in an unfamiliar lair

for decades

he rests

his dreams

wonders who he is, where he'd been
and his return to he

following

new lands flung wide and open

calling out to him, arousing, he set off

journey unbound by foot and sound
into high terrain

circling about, sniffing out his new identity
carving sand, overgrown claws digging his watchful holes

looking beyond
a fresh and warbled horizon

he marches out

head held high, strong back and legs now
no longer swayed

he wanders a trajectory

of

dirt carved caves and trails from others
smelling seductive scents

brush hills, dark valleys
he crosses far, birthing his colorful savage

in a land partitioned to dance

it smells good here, there's food he can eat and sol that
warms his belly

water abundant enough

he finally forgot
who the missus even was

he knows

adventures await each passing step

taking many more, that's right

and then
one day

he wandered in a different cave,
with many splendid colors

carvings and paintings from times passed down
a fresh pool of water to quench his scorched thirst

admiring views, he never knew magical creatures like this
exist

crouching down, bent knees, ears flat and forward too

he circled the pond's reflective silver glass
unsure of what he saw

he
wasn't
alone

who's that in there, in where
in here, with me now

smaller frame, longer lashes
softer fur too

with a cocked head turned under his
a gaze that locked for centuries

she sees in him
his canine history

she knows this is true
with blood dried on her tooth
not just one or two

she sees him for his ferocity

takes one to know one, as the story goes

within those lashes long and dark-ringed eyes
Justice Fire churns, burning and branding into him

She•sees•Him

he doesn't know
what it's like
to be met, yet

inside his very own skin

by blood-hungry canines
his rite of birth, accepted

animals instinctively are we

she steps forward
with enough bite and force to remind him of
himself

clawing and howls, snarls and, growls, ensue

her fierce-hearted eyes meet his, over and over each
playful roll

plunk and wrestle, nuzzle and play
they hissssss and snarl louder
each moment of the day

until

full on howls exist, blowing past all the bullshit

he stands stronger and taller now with his nose in upward
dog

unleashing his very truth

she reflected him, and he her too

the taste of blood desired, thick-sticky rich
frightening all the same

he knows

she will eat with him
exactly•what•he•kills

My second cent

One morning when the light of day was still, blue, and rising, I found myself in my best friend's house from high school, experiencing fantastic simultaneous events. Somewhat familiar and somewhat new, it all felt a bit like déjà vu. The house walls stood the same as 30 years ago, but the layout wasn't as before.

Guiding myself on this tour, I notice new vertical staircases leading up to children's rooms, built-on with tape it seemed, full of bright yellows, electric blues, magical fuchsia with fluffy bright white pillows and fluorescent green-shaggy carpets; everything tactile for every sense, posters shouting wild unicorns, winged dragons, other mythical creatures flitting about under purple suns with shimmery orange skies. "How frikkin' adorable," I silently consider among a shen-level nod to my friend's evolution.

Continuing to walk through other bedrooms, down hallways, winding new paths entirely free. I find my feet wiggling into cotton-candy colored, four-inch, very plush, long-strand carpet, burying my toes, softening my gate. I have arrived in the living room as an old, respected friend; no time has passed. I hear family tones echoing, occasional pitches and squeals in the not-so-far distance as the walls boom with jubilance and laughter. I wonder about the stories embedded in wall dust. I approach gently, closing my eyes, touching them to listen even deeper. Decades of support and unbending presence, loyal they stand.

Next, hearing the quickest pitter-pattering feet coming abruptly in my direction. Three furry creatures with fourteen legs, reaching my arms high, their furious speed zooming in from this hall and that, circling like they do when there is too much zing in their tails to stand still.

Then, I see my other best friend's pointed ears, a stately stance, and signature tufts sprouting from his ear base, my closest bud of 17 years, now scrambling past, hunched real low and crouched, trying to outrun these crazy beasts. Mr. ABC is orange and white, striped, with precious white boots on his paws and the longest, whitest, noble whiskers protruding from his gorgeous muzzle. I love his face. In this moment he was barely a blip on my radar.

I raised my authoritative voice at these new mongrels to break their focus and stop the madness. Busting up their natural state of fun to save exhaustion of my old man.

I notice the rest of the house has at once been extinguished; only Mr. ABC and I remain.

I carry on with sitting in my favorite recliner, then making dinner, while my mind-crafter creates and imagines exciting adventures into the evening, as if we were at home. We check on each other to see if one needs a lap warmer, snuggles, food, or play time, and then carry on some more.

When all movements hushed and finally settled... I noticed something different.

I saw he had a bump on his little pointy cheekbone. Taking a closer look, it didn't present as much of anything, really. I spread the skin taut for an even closer inspection that he allowed. Brushing and barber-pinning back his very long fur that Siberians are known for, I inspect and find nothing emergent. Weird.

As blue light became densely black and several new dawns passed, I noticed him sleeping more and more, curled up unusually like never before.

I reached for him to check in and notice his little ribs... "Wow, something is wrong". I roll him over, realize his limpness, and begin examining him like a protective lioness. I see his little cheekbone bump has now morphed into something I can't fix. Too much time has passed.

I pick him up in a strange yet familiar home where silence was deafening and judgmental "less than" moments strangle curiously. Now cradling Mr. ABC in my arms with a natural baby sway. Gentle and slow, side to side, left to right, and so it goes. No bouncing. Hoping that somehow it was soothing and I would discover what next to do.

I ponder options swiftly to save him. Remembering the prior rush, how could I have missed this injury? Simultaneously recalling that those mongrels, while not the same, reminded me of a different scrap he got into a few years earlier. For a few seconds, I feel very confused.

Were you in a fight before and not now? Where did these creatures go anyway?

Continuing to sway him back and forth in my arms, in a quandary. I continue to wander.

Why is my friend's house so silent now? Where did everyone go? I need help!

Flashes of our inter-species life together desperately whiz by as I feel his body softening and weakening in my grip. My tears begin to flow; my heart already knows.

Mr. ABC starts gently and slightly to twist himself from face down to paws up, wrenching and rolling all the way over in my careful cradle, dare I move? A stillness takes us both to somewhere new.

His roll becomes janky and awkward, his limbs thicken and lengthen right before my ever-living eyes. His belly becomes rounder and wider, his legs much longer too. His fur becomes fur-less skin, like human skin, and oh so smooth. His head extends and tremors itself into something else with non-tufted ears now, human eyes, a nose and mouth, whisker-free.

He has next-twisted into an adorable little, human boy, looking me square in the eye, with jubilance and glee, and shouts, "Do you want to play?!" in a high pitch only a 6-year-old could squeak.

Before I can answer, he springs out of my arms, lands on his two human feet, looks back at me for the chase, wiggling his tushy, and races off before I can even reach for him!

All at once.
Entire beliefs shed themselves free.

The next thing I know, I wake up from my night's sleep.
Disturbed.

Instantly back in this 3-D reality, feeling unspoken sacred insights.
Too real. Too deep. Too vibrant.

It feels like a potent wisdom nugget, direct learning, and a soul message, hand-delivered, on the edge of surrender and meaning making.

"This couldn't have been but a dream?"
What is the point of that?

Looking for meaning, I revisited a million times a second, the all too real feeling of Mr. ABC in my arms and I couldn't:

- do more

- be more

- fix it

- save my little guy

I found a form of self-hate. As if I was missing the presence of the moment to love him, unconditionally, in his transition.

This nugget revealed transformation as transitory nature, that lives upon us every second, when we choose to listen deeper, surrender, and open ourselves into the unknown.

My two cents:
Love is love and always constant.
It isn't pain, pleasure, or something wicked or even beautiful... love is the interwoven fabric of our true nature. Self-reflection, authenticity, presence, and honesty are cornerstones of self-love and loving unconditionally, like these two journeys of the wolf and Mr. ABC.

Growing up, I always questioned what unconditionally meant since it seemed over-used and transactional in my experience. I realize in this aftermath that the *action of transformation* and *every act of every change* are fundamental elements and opportunities of love for Self and Other. Suppose we allow and permit the ever-morphing, transformative true-nature of life deeply, in ourselves and for ourselves. In that case, I am convinced this is one of the most powerful ways we can remain eternally in love.

Love yourself through every up and down and sideways turn this rollercoaster of life presents... and know that you are inherently love at your core without doing or being anything. Remembering the range we carry and experience in ourselves is the range we hold and experience in others.

Love is love and always constant.

We are the gardens of compassion.

Crystal Clenney is an international storyteller, public speaker, intuitive, empath, owner of an enterprise payroll software consultancy, art broker, and founder of a platform called Intuitive Human©. Crystal never looked back after being spontaneously awakened by a three-hour L.I.S.T.E.N. experience at age twenty-five, which she describes as "...lighted shards of glass entering and healing my body." With her belief systems completely shattered, she began a focused mission to learn more about what happened, dedicating the next twenty years to studying energy medicine, natural healing, and cultivating and fine-tuning subtle levels of awareness. Today, Crystal excavates intuitive experiences globally, helping others unearth and integrate highly impactful, view-shifting intuitive events. Intuitive Human© discovers nuanced trends and patterns across eighteen intuitive tracks, defining the somatic signaling system and revealing how intuition is communicating in our bodies.

Attuning to intuition is like tuning the human instrument to play the best song of your life.

www.intuitivehuman.com/selflove

www.intuitivehuman.com

www.instagram.com/intuitive_human/

www.facebook.com/crystal.clenney/

www.youtube.com/channel/UC0X09SWRjnderchd7_-Piow

The Power of Self-Love

By Dr. Constance Leyland

Self-love is a transformative journey that transcends various aspects of my life. Whether as a professor, a mom, a wife, a director, a podcast host, or a business owner, each role brings unique challenges and opportunities for personal growth. As I explored the significance of self-love in these multifaceted roles, I learned to emphasize the importance of nurturing myself amidst diverse responsibilities and commitments.

Self-Love as a Professor:

As a professor, self-love involves recognizing and appreciating my expertise, knowledge, and teaching abilities. It means embracing my unique voice and contributions to academia. By valuing my achievements and continuous learning, I bolster my self-esteem and inspire my students to reach their full potential. Self-compassion allows me to embrace imperfections, learn from my mistakes, and create a supportive learning environment that fosters growth and success.

Self-Love as a Mom:

Being a mom demands tremendous emotional and physical energy. It is essential to prioritize self-love to ensure my well-being and provide the best care for my children. Self-love, as a mom, entails acknowledging my worth, setting boundaries, and embracing self-care practices. By nurturing my own needs, I model self-compassion and teach my children the importance of valuing themselves and creating a harmonious and loving environment for their growth.

Self-Love as a Wife:

Within marriage, self-love involves maintaining a sense of self while fostering a deep connection with my partner. It means honoring my individuality, dreams, and interests while nurturing open communication and trust. Self-love allows me to set boundaries, prioritize my well-being, and ensure a healthy balance between my personal growth and the growth of my relationship. I contribute to a stronger, more fulfilling partnership by loving and valuing myself.

Self-Love as a Director:

As a director, self-love is paramount in leading and inspiring others. It entails recognizing and appreciating my talents, skills, and achievements. Embracing my creativity and vision fosters a positive work environment, empowering my team to reach their full potential. Practicing self-acceptance allows me to learn from failures, grow as a leader, and make impactful decisions with confidence. By cultivating self-love, I enhance my effectiveness as a director and create a culture of empowerment and growth.

Self-Love as a Podcast Host:

As a podcast host, self-love is integral to delivering authentic and meaningful content. It involves embracing my unique voice, ideas, and perspectives. By valuing my worth and knowledge, I create a platform where listeners can find inspiration, education, and entertainment. Self-love allows me to overcome self-doubt, embrace vulnerability, and connect deeply with my audience. By nurturing my passion for storytelling, I create a positive impact and inspire others to cultivate self-love in their own lives.

Self-Love as a Business Owner:

As a business owner, self-love plays a vital role in achieving success and maintaining a healthy work-life balance. It involves acknowledging my accomplishments, taking pride in my entrepreneurial journey, and valuing my skills and expertise. Practicing self-care and setting boundaries enable me to navigate challenges with resilience and maintain my passion for my business. By prioritizing self-love, I create a positive company culture, inspire my employees, and foster a sustainable and thriving business.

The Power of Self-Love:

Regardless of our roles, self-love is a transformative force that enhances our overall well-being and effectiveness. By cultivating self-love, we set a positive example for others, encourage personal growth, and inspire those around us to embrace their own self-worth.

The Power of Self-Love
By Dr. Constance Leyland

Dr. Leyland is an accomplished academic with a distinguished career spanning over a decade as a Professor, Dean of Universities, Podcast Host, and International Published Author. With a passion for education and a commitment to intellectual growth, Dr. Leyland has made significant contributions to the academic community and beyond.

As a Professor, Dr. Leyland has nurtured the minds of countless students, inspiring them to pursue knowledge and critical thinking. Their expertise lies in business and they have successfully imparted their deep understanding of the subject matter to their students through engaging lectures, thought-provoking discussions, and innovative teaching methods. Dr. Leyland's dedication to education has earned them the respect and admiration of both peers and students alike.

In addition to their teaching responsibilities, Dr. Leyland has assumed leadership roles as a Dean of Universities. Their visionary approach and effective management skills have brought about positive changes, fostering academic excellence and creating an environment conducive to learning and research. Under their guidance, the universities have flourished, attracting talented faculty and students from around the world.

Recognizing the importance of disseminating knowledge beyond the confines of the classroom, Dr. Leyland has embraced the realm of podcasting. As a Podcast Host, they bring insightful conversations, expert interviews, and thought-provoking discussions to a global audience. Their podcast has become a platform for intellectual exchange, where experts from various fields come together to explore cutting-edge ideas and address critical issues.

Furthermore, Dr. Leyland is an internationally published author, with their works making a significant impact on the academic community. Their research and publications have garnered recognition and praise, contributing to the advancement of knowledge in their field. Through their written works, Dr. Leyland has shaped the scholarly discourse and provided valuable insights to fellow researchers, students, and professionals worldwide.

Dr. Leyland's dedication to academia, leadership acumen, captivating podcasting skills, and impactful written contributions make them respected and influential figures in their field. They continue to inspire and empower others through their teaching, administrative roles, podcasting, and scholarly endeavors, leaving an indelible mark on the intellectual landscape.

Embracing My Heart

By Amy Nicastro-Clark

I didn't know my body and mind were so connected when I was young. I didn't realize my body would take on the pains of my poor decisions and hold on to them for life. I worked so hard to protect my heart; a bulldozer could not set it free. I was on guard from an early age. Oh! How my body would hold on to the past and choices I was unwilling to let go of. My mind would swirl thoughts of the past around in my head over and over. I would obsess over who did what to me. I was a victim of my circumstances because I allowed myself to be that. I had no idea how to take a stand for myself, and I thought it was all to do with my hair. What we think about, we bring about.

A tussle began again after I wrote my *Align, Attract, Accept, and Accelerate Abundance* chapter. My chapter was *Allowance vs. Resistance*. What an invitation. The thing I resisted most was self-care and I invited it in. Language is everything. How do I fight myself? Let me count the ways. I know I do well for my physical and mental well-being when I eat less and exercise more. Add meditation and I am golden. Finding the balance has been a task. I wait for the right time or day to start. Once I start and get in the groove, I am on it. I move mountains, and then I get to the point of almost... and I stop. That's the chokehold and knowing is half the battle. Why?

Self Care is not selfish when I can love myself enough to build and stick to the habit. I remember my desire to be thinner than my high school boyfriend, Hercules. I wanted to appear thinner than him so we looked hot walking down the hallways. I accomplished it. Surface looks were so important to me. I could look the part of any role I played, from high school, girlfriend, biker chick, thin and leather, to a mother. It was easy until common sense got in the way. I married that high school boy, twice boy, and we had children in both marriages, three total. I proved to myself anything was possible.

Now I had to find the time around other people's schedules to take care of me. Three days of no physical activity, and I was a time bomb. It was definitely easier to stay motivated once I was separated and had an outside reason. I clearly wanted to show my husband what he was missing. I would work out, have breakfast with the children, and then head off to the park, where I would "bump" into him on purpose. They got their fill of their Dad, and I hoped he would love me enough to stop drinking and come home. Well, that was far-fetched. I was not the issue or the answer. A person needs to love themself enough to love others, so my journey of self-love grew deeper.

Self-care is not selfish. Like many women, I thought I had to give up my own needs for the sake of others, at least the women I knew. It has been a continuous journey to love myself. Logically I do, wholeheartedly I do! Then something puts the brakes on, and things I know work seem to stop working. I used to crawl out of bed, sneakers nearby, dressed in my leotard, yes leotard, turn the tv to a workout with my workout buddy, Bess Motta, a woman with hair like mine, for 20 minutes, after a month enhanced, led to the first 10 minutes to warm-up, a mile run, then, return to the last 10 min workout and cool down. I was thrilled when it came out on video, and I always go back to this workout, now on Youtube. In high school, I designed my own workout to Gloria Stevens moves, playing side one of the Saturday Night Fever album. To this day, I want to get down on all fours when I hear it playing in a store. It makes me giggle how that side of the album worked in front of the mirror until my brother took the record needle to it. It was a daily habit and it was fun.

Portraying a Know-it-All made life challenging. I knew more than my mother, listened to my father, and was sure I was all set by sophomore year in high school for whatever life dealt me. I was too cool for school and had a business making people feel good. I was a non-cigarette smoker carrying a pack of Marlboro filled with the special smokes I liked. It made the day go fast, as if that was the reason.

I never wanted to go to college. I only wanted to grow up and have children and treat them the way I wanted to be treated. I did not allow teasing, I didn't lie to them. I showed up, and I knew what they were doing. We communicated and I was honored to parent them. I made sure they were fed and had the best of the best. I even stayed friends with their father, a man I will always love from a distance because he gave me everything I ever wanted, little humans.

I had years of running before I married the man I loved. Decisions I allowed others to make for me tore me apart. A baby at 15 was not in the cards for my mother and me. She had six and was clear raising mine was not an option. It's a miracle I am here. The pain was so real, and there was no going back. I beat myself up for years. My shrink called me a Poly-Addict. I would put anything in front of me to feel good. Pop it and forget it. Except I couldn't really forget it. It was more like shoot it and nod out. I wanted to feel nothing. I ran to the instant effect. Nobody forced me. I asked to shoot heroin, and I didn't stop because I didn't like it anymore. Seeing my aging father and wanting him to be proud of me, I knew this was not my path. I stopped because my father never gave up on me, and he gave me the strength to see myself differently. I am grateful to love my father enough to see him as my idol. Then, I never gave up on him. He was always my savior. He gave me my healing, loving spirit. My mother gave me tenacity, wisdom, and the longing to become a soft pillow. When he died, our three weeks in hospice, he left me in peace. I honor him by keeping that peace in my body.

I am grateful to be the best version of both and have created a legacy in their names; Parents **Are The Key 501(c)(3).** My mother founded the Head Start Program with Communities United in Lexington, MA. A single mother of six with a man who always said yes to anything she said no to. She did not have it easy, and I contributed to her hard. She is my gift, and he is my present. I am forever grateful for their love, regardless of how it was given. Each had their wisdom to share, and emotions were not a welcome thing in the seventies. I finally got my father's message, "Get your heart in touch with your intellect." One he had said for years that I could not hear, when I finally could hear, mountains began to move. Trust the process, trust myself.

I did a women's weekend in 2014. That weekend allowed me to start to chisel the stone protecting my heart, slowly letting go of my tomboy persona while holding on to my relationship with my father. He was my rock and learned how to be with my mother.

Once I accepted my parents for who they were in the world, I could find my self-acceptance. Nothing was about me. They were children when they got married and took on the world. I accepted them and how they shaped me, and I love them both wholeheartedly. Then, I began the journey of accepting myself! The tools I got from my weekend were priceless.

My two cents about my self-care. How I take care of myself is how I take care of everything. Proximity is key, find your circle. Find women you can trust and give them your crap, holding it in it kills us. Slow down, look around and feel nature. I Meditate till I can be still. Meditation is a very personal, individual practice and journey. Much like Yoga. Allow the gift of stillness, and I don't stop until I embrace it. I found as much as I couldn't; I could. Trusting myself, gave me my relationship with the Universe that leads me where I am supposed to be. When I began loving myself, the rest began to come, and my mind found rest when it set my heart free. I learned that words matter. Mindfully let go of try, but, and if. The piece of myself I once ran from was now out, my heart.. The tomboy I was, was now ready to meet the woman I had become. Wholeheartedly.

Amy Nicastro-Clark is a Serial Entrepreneur and Inventor that would give the world away. The lessons she learned have taught many that giving is the best drug. Self-care is not selfish. It is a necessary part of life to succeed in all our relationships, especially with ourselves. How I take care of myself is how I take care of everything.

Native of Brookline, Massachusetts, Daughter of Cosmo D. Nicastro Jr. and Elizabeth Nicastro, two people who met very young and looked to live the American Dream having child after child. Sibling to 5, and grateful to all of them for teaching me resilience and strength, something I never thought I could have. Mother of 3 exceptional adult children and Grammy of 4 so far. Aidan, Jack, Lena, and Arlo. Grateful to be a part of this amazing group of writers. A Platinum Partner of Tony Robbins finishing a year of amazing growth and ready to share the wisdom. A healer at heart, who learned Giving is the best drug there is.

https://www.facebook.com/amy.n.clark.7

http://www.parentsarethekey.org

https://www.linkedin.com/in/1localidea/

https://podcasts.apple.com/us/podcast/thriving-in-recovery/id1655042905?i=1000615141853

https://www.mothersagainstaddiction.org/

Perfectly Imperfect

By Rebekah O'Dell

Love Yourself. Your life depends on it. If anyone is an expert on this topic, it is me. I have gone through most of my life not feeling good enough and feeling like I have to be perfect for others to love me. The abandonment issues began early on when my parents divorced and my father signed away his rights. My mom remarried a month after I turned six to a man who was widowed with four boys. Overnight I went from being an only child to being the oldest of five, and the only girl. For years I felt out of place and like I didn't belong. A deep-rooted belief was created that for me to belong, I needed to fit in and make others happy so that they would want and love me. Little did I know then that constantly pleasing people was depleting my energy and setting me up for disappointment. I was so afraid that others would not accept me and that they would leave me, which is exactly what I experienced growing up in relationships, over and over again.

I became a chameleon in order to fit in, and due to my deep empathic abilities, matching other people's energies and helping them feel better became my defense mechanism. This led to many people calling me their best friend, all the while, I never felt like any of them actually knew the real me. And anytime I let her come out and shine, I felt misunderstood. I could tap into others and understand them because I could feel them while dissociating from my feeling of self. I then turned to substance abuse and became the master of fitting in. I had friends in every category. But I felt so alone and misunderstood. I became so hard on myself to be a perfect version. I obsessively worked out my body and thought my looks measured my desirability. I became so insecure that I couldn't make eye contact with people if I had a zit on my face! I would nitpick and criticize everything about myself and take people's comments personally. People would comment on how skinny I was and ask If I was anorexic. Little did they know, I ate like a racehorse and never put on a pound. I hated how skinny I was. I felt like a 12-year-old girl or felt like I had a little boy body while in my twenties, and all I wanted was to feel like a woman. Because of my self-worth issues, I allowed myself to be abused by others because I was emotionally abusing myself.

I became very promiscuous and sought out the wrong kind of attention, chasing the feeling of being wanted. This resulted in a series of unhealthy relationships and teen pregnancies, resulting in a miscarriage at the age of 17. At the age of 19 I gave birth to my son, which saved my life because at the time I found out I was pregnant with him, I had been using drugs, drinking and smoking, and quit cold turkey the day I found out I was pregnant. His father however continued to use drugs, as well as abuse me for the next year.

It was around this time I started receiving energy healing and learned that I am not defined by my past. I learned that I deserved to be happy and loved and that it began with how I was treating and loving myself. This empowered me to leave the relationship when my son was a year and a half old and began my journey as a single mother. I realized there was no way I wanted him to learn that behavior nor grow up in that environment. I wanted him to grow up loving himself.

It wasn't until in my late twenties that I realized I needed to *really* love myself. When my son was six, I married the man of my dreams. This relationship was actually healthy and brought to light all of my unhealthy patterns and deep-rooted limiting beliefs. One evening my husband came into the bathroom as I washed the makeup off my face and hid from him so he wouldn't think I was ugly. He said, " I feel like you aren't being honest in our relationship because you always try to hide your flaws. I didn't marry you because you were perfect. I don't expect you to be perfect. You can't make me happy. Only I can make myself happy. I don't need you but I enjoy spending time with you; you are like the icing on my cake."

Now I am leaving out a lot of context to my life story and all of the things in between, but in my mind, I had no idea how I had attracted such an amazing husband who was so strong in his sense of self that he could be a great example of self-love and was willing to call me out. At that moment, I decided I needed to face my fears and take my many masks off. For the next few years I forced myself to become vulnerable and allow my husband and others to see me without makeup. I started writing love letters of everything I wished others would say to me. I began putting my needs before others, and before long, people who I thought were my friends began to fall away. I became intolerant of fake people as I was no longer being fake. And then, I began pursuing my passion for helping others find themselves, dove deeper into my healing, and uncovered hidden parts of myself.

As a 39-year-old, I can finally say I truly love myself. The journey was long, as I had a lot to rewire. But I no longer feel the need to people please and blend in to feel loved. I no longer value superficial looks and materialistic aspects of life. I now attract people who fall in love on a soul level because I love myself on a soul level. I allow myself to be vulnerable and in turn this creates safety and trust in my relationships. Communicating my needs and boundaries with others and prioritizing me time, sets a high standard of the type of people and situations I allow myself to experience. This is a surefire way to know who respects me and who doesn't.

To truly love myself, I must put my needs before others. I can't give from an empty cup. My number one priority daily is to fill my cup up. This means filling my body's life force energy with things that nourish my spirit and bring me joy. This is walking in nature first thing every morning, talking to the trees, sun, and the birds, Doing my morning sadhana of kundalini breathwork, yoga, and meditation. Journaling, singing, and dancing. Pulling cards and then eating foods that excite and comfort me. This way, I am grounded and rooted in my sense of self and can navigate the daily challenges with a clear mind and heart, and I get to be creative, find solutions, and imagine new possibilities. This also means I no longer desire to do things that bring my energy down. For example, I quit drinking and going to the bars. I quit spending time around people who thrive off of gossip and drama. I am only interested in others who are filling their cups up. That way, we never deplete one another or are codependent and instead have healthy relationships that inspire and support.

Knowing my boundaries has been one of the biggest lessons I have had to learn, and is still a work in progress. However by practicing them, I have been able to develop trust in my ability to say no and stand up for myself. I am not perfect at it and noticed when I am depleted, tired and stressed out, this is my body's way of telling me I have been slacking with my self care and need to take time out. An analogy I recently came up with has helped me clarify and recognize boundaries and I have shared it with a few people;

"I will no longer give my cookies away for free. I can share with you my recipes and show you how I make mine, but you have to do the work to create yours. Go out and buy the ingredients and spend time practicing your recipes. Then we can trade cookies as friends. If you don't want to do that, then you can pay me for my time and service as a client. Only when I am overflowing with cookies, can I choose to donate them for free. "

Self Acceptance goes hand in hand with self love. I have finally come to accept myself as is, Perfectly Imperfect. I realize I am getting older every day and do not want to waste any more time beating myself up, and choose to follow my joy whenever it's possible. I get to decide how to express my creativity through my aesthetic. It's a fun process. No longer needing approval from others is liberating. I get to be all I want and more. I deserve this. And so do you.

Love,

Rebekah

Rebekah O'Dell is experienced in the art of embracing who you are, even in your mess, and facilitating others to do the same by helping them to recognize their beauty and cultivate healthy, nurturing relationships with themselves. She is passionate about holistic wellness and creating ceremonies. She loves bringing people together in nature with the spirit of unity and diversity. She is on a mission to empower people with sovereignty and raise the vibration and consciousness of our planet so that we can expand and grow into our fullest potential as divine star beings. Rebekah is a multi-preneur and is trailblazing a spiritual path for business. She is co-creator of Full Moon Camping Retreats, LLC, where she is in the fifth year of facilitating transformational life experiences with her brother in the four corners area of the U.S. She currently resides in the White Mountains of AZ, where she owns and operates the Spirit Glow Holistic Salon and Spirit Grove Healing Sanctuary, LLC, and is a collaborating member of the White Mountain Healing Alliance. Rebekah is a seasoned Cosmetologist of 21 years, a Master Instructor of

Integrated Energy Therapy®, a Reiki Master Teacher in Usui® and Holy Fire®, and holds multiple yoga and life coaching certifications. She loves guiding others to do what she does, whether in one on one sessions or behind the chair, in classes or workshops training holistic entrepreneurs, hosting business masterminds, or facilitating retreats.

www.fullmooncampingretreats.com

www.rebekahsrealm.com

IG & FB

@ fullmooncampingretreats

@ rebekahsrealm

There Are Two Of Us

By Suzy Belcher

In rehab, someone told me, "Secrets keep you sick."

I decided to go to rehab, and it was the best decision I ever made. I was at the stage where, every day, I would wake up wanting more, hoping for more, and asking for more. More never came, and then I asked myself another question.

Do I want to live, or do I want to end it all?

It all began when I was sent off to weekly boarding school. I was four years old. I couldn't understand why I was being sent away. I thought there was something wrong with me. A few days into this new school, we all sat down to have lunch when this terrifying voice screamed from behind me, "If you can't learn to live in a right-handed world, you don't deserve to eat your food" – I am left-handed. So, I was sent out of the dining room in front of 600 students.

I was then sent off to boarding school in the UK on my own at 12 years old. I had never traveled to another country alone and was placed as an unaccompanied minor. My safety was in the hands of a stranger. It was the very first exeat weekend at this new school where all the students could go home, and a parent asked the house mistress what was happening to "that girl from Africa". The house mistress replied that I was to stay at the school as my parents had not given the school any instructions. Luckily the Parent took me in and I became her daughter's best friend. We are still the best of friends today.

Whatever I did, it never seemed good enough for my mother. She never wanted to have anything to do with me. I was sent away as if I was a hindrance, and it had a massive impact on me. My Father worked and traveled extensively but was certainly my rock throughout my life. He saw how my mother handled me. I am not here to lay blame or accuse anyone of anything, as these events have made me who I am today.

These events impacted me, as I am sure they would on anyone. Rejection, low self-worth, and insecurities controlled who I was. The more I tried, the more Mum pushed me away, and whatever I seemed to do, we just could not have a relationship that was love, compassion, or acceptance.

I left home when I was 16. I got into the Film Industry. It was glamorous and exciting and filled with effervescent energy. I felt at home, living out of a suitcase, not getting too embedded in any relationships that could judge me. I was on the run.

Back then, the film industry was renowned for working hard but also playing hard, and I played hard. It made me feel alive and accepted and of course, it suppressed all the hurt within. I didn't know this at the time, though. So on I went with my life, getting deeper and deeper into addiction. It got so bad that I could not operate without "fixing" myself every morning.

I persistently asked myself if I wanted to continue living at that stage. I kept self-sabotaging in the most shocking ways. I even caused an accident that split my face in half. I hated myself so much that I couldn't live with it.

So that is when I asked myself If I wanted to continue living or if I should end it.

I spoke to my father and told him that I wanted to go to rehab. He made it happen. I was 35 years old. My mother accompanied me down to South Africa. I checked into rehab, and my life actually started then. I learned to stand up for myself. I learned to control my emotions. I learned to cope. I learned how to set boundaries. I learned how to start loving myself for me. There was an incident where my mother stormed into a group meeting and screamed at me in front of everyone, and I dealt with it. I didn't run.

After rehab, there was a confidence that had been created within me. One that I had never known and although it took a while, nothing would hold me back.

My darling father passed away in December 2007. In March 2008, something happened! I received an email from my sister-in-law. It was from a colleague of her mother's, and she said, "Hello, I have been battling cancer, and I am looking for information regarding my birth mother . I want to understand if there is cancer in the family to see if it is hereditary. My mother's maiden name is Jane Fairclough*, and my name is Suzanne."

I could not believe that this was happening. It was my mother's name, AND the email sender bore the same name and spelling as I have.

I was in total shock, and at the next meeting with Mum, my siblings and myself asked her if this was true. She admitted it was and that she had fallen pregnant out of wedlock in the 50'S. She had been placed in a nunnery to have the child and then, through a pre-arranged adoption, the baby was adopted by a family who had worked with Mum.

As soon as we opened up, the shock of this 53-year-old secret made my mother slam the emotional gates shut, demanding that we never speak about this again. Mum had always been a conflicted soul, and I believe she suffered greatly.

I went to meet Suzanne. I traveled across to Australia, and as I walked out of the arrivals gate in Sydney airport, I zoned in on an exact replica of my mother, only 30 years younger. It was surreal.

Three days into this extremely emotional meeting with a sister I didn't know existed, something else happened. I had been left alone on this small holding in the "outback" as Suzanne had gone to work. Suzanne asked me if I would lock up the chickens in the evening, as there were Dingos about. Of course, the girl from Africa said yes.

So off I went at dusk to lock up the chickens and was confronted by a "big red" Kangaroo. He locked onto me and we had what seemed like a 15-minute fight. He wanted to kill me! I fought with all my might and finally got away from him. I survived, but only because I didn't give in. I chose to fight for my life for the second time in my life. In both these incidents where I decided to fight for something, it was divine guidance that shaped my decision. During the Kangaroo attack, it was the most vivid voice telling me to "do what you would do in a dog attack" over and over again. It was my Father who taught me that 30 years earlier. It is what saved me that day.

It all made sense why Mum had been so negative to me. I believe that she subconsciously compared me to the "Suzanne" she gave away, which wounded her for her entire life. All of the conflict my mother felt was not because she was a negative, spiteful person. Perhaps it was because she was comparing me with the child that she gave away.

Mum was given an opportunity to heal from the pain that she lived with most of her life. The secret that she lived with. She chose not to. When I look back at all the signs, it was evident that there was something that had impacted her.

I chose to heal from the pain that was created by someone else's pain. It took me on a journey through addiction, self-loathing, and doubt. It was the safari that I had to take to get to where I am today.

Today, I take people on Safaris and Retreats in Africa using revolutionary coaching techniques that help create unlimited possibilities for your lives by using Africa's wild intellectual knowledge, empowering you to reinvent yourselves.

Through my vast knowledge of Africa and its people, I offer unique coaching techniques based on methods from the continent's flora and fauna that will transform the perspective completely. I provide an exciting opportunity to uncover new pathways toward success in life while providing valuable insight into how we can think differently about potential challenges not found elsewhere.

If you are looking for a reliable partner in reinvention, I have the expertise and passion you need to take charge of creating progress in your life with conviction! My mission is to inspire others to look beyond what they thought was possible so they can unlock their true potential and find authentic happiness within themselves. My vision is one where every woman feels empowered through understanding both their strengths as well as areas of growth, so they have more control over the path they choose for their future success!

There is always more to any story. We can choose to live in someone else's pain or stand up and live our truth.

Suzy Belcher is a revolutionary coach that helps women create unlimited possibilities for their lives by using Africa's wild intellectual knowledge, empowering them to reinvent themselves. Through her vast knowledge of Africa and its people, she offers unique coaching techniques based on methods from the continent's flora and fauna that will transform your perspective completely. She provides an exciting opportunity to uncover new pathways toward success in your life while providing valuable insight into how you can think differently about potential challenges that you won't find anywhere else. If you are looking for a reliable partner in reinvention, Suzy Belcher has the expertise and passion you need to take charge of creating progress in your life with conviction! Her mission is to inspire others to look beyond what they thought was possible so they can unlock their true potential and find authentic happiness within themselves. Her vision is one where every woman feels empowered through understanding both their strengths as well as areas of growth, so they have more control over the path they choose for their future success!

Social Media Handles:

Facebook:https://www.facebook.com/SuzyBelcher/

Instagram:https://www.instagram.com/suzysuccess/

Linkedin:https://www.linkedin.com/in/suzybelcher/

Love Yourself and The World Will Follow

By Sid McNairy

Have you taken a moment to look at love? Have you looked at how much you love yourself? Where does self-love start? Where does self-love get lost? Have you wondered why the world seems to need more love? These questions arise when the concept of "Self Love" becomes a daily practice.

Self-love, by definition, is a state of acceptance and appreciation of oneself that expands from actions that support one's physical, psychological, and spiritual growth.

"This above all: to thine own self be true,
And it must follow, as the night the day,
Thou canst not then be false to any
man." -William Shakespeare

As viewed in William Shakespeare's words, when love of self is experienced, love from outside will follow. Just as one can see, as the night comes, the day is soon to follow. Love of the self will bring forward a greater love in every way.

As time has passed, it has become clear that Peace is the launch pad that allows all to access love. When Peace is lost, love is not accessible. Look at life and see how love appears to be gone when Peace is lost. Peace is the access point to love.

Peace will continue to be the birthplace of love in one's life. On the journey to self-love, take the time to find Peace to bring forward love in every way. One will see how to build love all around by seeing where Peace is lost. Self-love will come forward at the place where love has been given away. This will continue to present itself in the reality of the beholder based on one's personal relationship to Peace in any moment.

Sometimes, things move in a direction away from self-love in life. Life creates moments where relationships are ending, and one can examine why the relationships are moving in the direction ahead. To access self-love, one must hold themselves accountable for where they are willing to sacrifice Peace. Once a look inside has taken place, it is possible to move forward with greater access to love.

A big lesson to grasp along the way is that Peace is the access point to love. It is easy to see that when Peace is lost, love leaves the moment at hand. When a person is in an argument, can they be in love? Only if an inner experience of peace is maintained will the argument move from a place of love. This is the same experience taking place within us all with self-love. Capturing inner Peace allows self-love to come to the forefront.

Here are two practices that can enhance the experience of self-love.

Know Thyself:

Grab a journal and draw a line down the middle and a line across the middle. In the top left, list five of your faults. Use a single word to describe them in a list.

Underneath in the bottom left corner, write the opposite to each one you wish to embody in single words. Now in the top right corner, directly across from your faults, write what is gained by those faults. For example, an angry person may experience a sense of protection or feel heard. There is something received from each fault, which is why one continues to access them.

In the bottom right corner of the grid, compose a list next to the positive desired characteristics of one's faults. Use single words to describe the weakness of each word. When one is too much of anything, it simply is too much. If a person is too kind, they will often be weak. A person who is too lighthearted may be naive. Find the strengths in the faults and the weakness of the perceived positive characteristics.

From this, start to see how one can fall in love with all expressions of oneself. Take the time to see how to be appropriate in every way. Learn to move from the strengths of the faults and the positive characteristics. Here lies the opportunity to gain a greater view of cultivating self-love. By coming into the awareness of being appropriate in one's actions, one will be able to let go of the good or bad and experience the self with divine love.

Look in the Mirror:

This lesson is simple and yet profound. Find a mirror, look in the mirror, and look into your eyes. Take seven breaths and pause as you gaze into your own eyes. Breathe in, and feel Peace within. Now, with each breath out, say, "I love you" with your breath. Seven times. Continue this exercise for ten days, at least twice daily, and notice the difference. Repeat as often as needed until self-love has been captured.

Everyone experiences the environment differently. Our environment will continue to cultivate love within or take it away. It's time to take responsibility for your own experiences. As a baby, my mother put mirrors with toys on every side of my crib. Whenever someone would want to take me out of the crib, I would cry. I learned early on that I love being with me. It was easy then, as the baby in the mirror was truly the only one like me.

Take this exercise and fall in love with you. The reflection that grows from within will attract one from the outer world, reflecting what is within. Love yourself through the practice of reflection and watch all come through. In the Native American teachings, it is in walking the red road that all is done. When looking at the meanings of directions, South is about one's personal reflection and seeing the divine in all. Take a look in a calm body of water. What will be seen? One sees their reflection. Humans are made of mostly water, somewhere around 60% water. Because of this, when looking at another individual, one sees and experiences oneself.

Find peace within, and allow love to be birthed. See love grow and watch how the inner world mirrors the outer. Everything is an internal protection of what is going on in the reality of what is happening in front of you.

Practice, practice, practice. This thing called life is a practice. Take the time to practice self-love, and continue to perfect the love of oneself. Self-love is the vehicle for the transformation of all things around the self. Every single human has the opportunity to elevate from where they are, and self-love is a huge part. Where energy is placed, energy grows. What you see is what you get. Go in and cultivate a space of peace that allows the creation of a deeper sense of love in life.

The Simple Keys to Self-love:

"Self-awareness" is the first key along the way to self-love. When coming into a state of self-love, be aware of how one is either loving the self or connecting to some form of fear. Coming from the knowledge that only love is real means that anything else is an illusion. The practice of self-love begins with the awareness of what is real and what illusions one has created within the mind.

"Inner Peace" is the second key. Create peace on the inside and allow it to shine through. Peace is the access point to love. Because of this, it is the place to allow love to grow for the self. Look in and know where peace is on the inside. Allow it to grow until 100% Peace resides within. The one who brings Peace sees love increase.

"Honor the word" is the third key. Words create the reality seen. Let the words expressed bring forward what is a desired outcome. Take the time to honor the words: thought, spoken, and expressed. Words paint the picture by honoring the word, one will create the reality one wishes to see.

"Practice, practice, practice" Loving oneself is the final key. By looking at life as a practice, know that you are strengthening what is coming. Bring forward discipline and see how all things mirror the consistency cultivated on the inside. How one does anything trickles into how one does everything. See how behaviors have been set in motion and what can come from a shift within. Practice self-love until loving oneself becomes unconscious. Love yourself, and the world will follow.

The journey is of self-love, it's a journey of love, and we are all one. In knowing "the Law of the One" by Rah, all goes back to the one. For one to love another is to love thyself. Loving one's self is to love another. We are all one.

Love thyself and **the world** will follow.

Love the world as one loves oneself.

Sid McNairy's track record speaks for itself. Since 1992 Sid has been changing lives and a conduit to thousands achieving their hearts' desires and living their dream life. Sid is here to help all RISE into their highest possibility. Sid's life is an example of how Real Impact Supports Everyone. To know Sid is to know how support for all is possible and is the way for all to receive love unconditionally.

"He Who Brings Peace" Sid McNairy sparks peace wherever he goes. The Warrior Within only allows for peace in any space he enters. Winning follows naturally as Sid transforms every part of his life to mirror Divine perfection. He's won as an internationally bestselling author of several life-changing books. He's won as a football and life coach who guides NFL, NBA athletes, and others into successful lives in the game of life. And he wins as a warrior-monk leader on the stage and in the yoga studio. In cultivating "The Art of Peaceful Living" community alongside his twin flame, the love of his life, and wife Liz, Sid offers the world a lighthouse for self-discovery grounded in the power of peace. He is a living testament to all he teaches, showing the world with his daily words and accomplishments, "Peace is the power to live by. Win at everything!" Sid is a story of the ModernMonk.

Sid has never pursued a path, simply allowing life and relations to call him forward to what's next. On March 7, 2023, Sid responded to his most recent request. Sid has said yes to moving forward with a 2028 presidential campaign. It's time!

To learn more about Sid, you can visit:

www.artofpeacefulliving.com

www.sidmcnairy.com

Instagram: Sidmcnairy

Facebook: https://www.facebook.com/sidmcnairy/

An Alien With Extra-ordinary Abilities

By Connie Osterholt

My official status on my VISA is an alien with extra-ordinary abilities, and I quite like it. Not the alien part so much, but the extra-ordinary abilities. The real reason I like it so much is because it's different. It sets me apart. I always felt different my whole life.

And those who were seen dancing were thought to be insane by those who could not hear the music.- Nietzsche

I'm one of three, and my older sister and younger brother required a lot of attention. I have always been good in school, good in sports, lots of friends, and very different from my siblings. I was treated very differently. Some asked if I felt I got shorted or lacked love and care. Not at all. It gave me freedom. I felt different in school, too, it was easy for me to study, and I had many friends. However, I never quite fit in.

I was very tall early on, and the boys I liked came to my shoulders. I was very shy and introverted, which sometimes seemed lonely. I loved sports and was quite good at it, but being good at things also set me apart and made me feel different. I was not quite like anybody else. I felt that I was born into the wrong family or was adopted. I wanted to be like my friends and schoolmates.

It was harder for me to love myself because I thought there was a mold very different from who I was.

156

Now, I know it's my uniqueness I came to embrace, appreciate, and even build a career on. I learned to love myself even if I didn't fit the mold. I can love other people so easily. I usually see the good and the bad, but I can love them anyway. That's easy for me, but to love myself.

I thought being critical of myself was a good thing. It gave me drive and motivation. I thought I might not be smart, talented, or skilled enough for many, many different reasons. I judged myself and it was picked up by others. Therefore I tried harder.

In my twenties, I was hanging out with a group of semi-veteran rowers who had been rowing together since they were students. I started rowing as well, and I did okay. The group wanted to go to the World Championships, and I wanted to do that as well. One rower asked me to row in a skiff together and enter the championship. Others told me I never could be good enough; I had only been rowing for one year! If I felt like I was lacking, and they confirmed.

People are like radio stations. We broadcast what we're thinking, what we're feeling, and what we are experiencing. Other people pick this up without really knowing and react to it. I put out that I might not be good enough for a lot of things. This signal was picked up by other people who responded to it and said, "Yeah, she is right; forget about her. She can never do that". I did not like hearing that from someone else. I entered the World Championship, rowing in a skiff. We ended last, but I did it! I was so proud that I did it despite all the comments.

Self-love has to do with rules about what's perfect, what's good enough, what's not perfect, what's not good enough, and how much perfection I need. If I am critical of myself, how can I love myself, not being perfect?

First, I started respecting myself. I appreciate myself for everything I can, everything I do, how I am, and how I react towards others. I respect what I do and what I give to the world, my friends, and my kids. I started respecting everything that I am and everything that I do.

I started to honor myself. My upbringing taught me to give and give but never to myself; that would be selfish. Soon, I gave from that empty place, and people felt it. So finally, I realized that it's important to honor myself. It's important to give to myself. It's important to take care of myself. It's important to take rest and do nothing if I choose, or sit in the sand and stare at the ocean, have a beach walk, be in beautiful nature, read, listen to beautiful music, or have silly conversations and giggles.

At first, I saw these things as ineffective use of my time. I felt that time should be spent being there for other people, making things work, building a career, and making money to take care of your family, kids, mom, dad, spouse, and friends. I felt I had to spend all my time doing and being there for others. When I started putting myself in the mix, honored myself, and realized how hard I worked, I knew I needed to re-energize. I needed to recuperate. Sometimes I needed to heal and take time off. I realized I needed to have more balance. Downtime is necessary to ensure I am healthy, vibrant, and energetic.

I no longer think it is selfish if I do something for myself, sleep in, take a long bath, or do any indulgent things labeled selfish growing up. I've learned that it is a balance, not selfishness. Honoring myself, respecting myself, and taking care of myself as well as taking care of other people, is self-love. I make sure that I am in the best state physically, emotionally, and mentally to take care of myself and everything important in my life with the energy to do so.

In general, I have a fairly good diet most of the time. I drink enough water and exercise regularly. I make time for my spiritual practices, resting, relaxing, recuperating, and spending time with other people. I do everything that makes me feel good so I am in the best state to care for others and myself. I must continually learn to love, respect, and honor myself, no matter my goals! I don't allow my goals to postpone me taking care of myself and loving myself. I love myself regardless! I love myself as I love my best friend. I love myself and am realistic enough to know that I'm imperfectly perfect.

Being in the best possible emotional and physical state helps me take care of myself. It helps me care for others and make a difference in the world, which is very important to me. I choose to be present and in awareness. I have learned that my state, emotion, and mood are not things that simply happen. I have influence! When I learned to take control of how I want to feel and find a way to get there, I can live in a beautiful state of Happiness most of the time.

I decided I wanted to be happy no matter what.

We are creatures of all emotions. It wouldn't be fair to choose only one and disregard every other emotion. I may be irritated or frustrated, sad or hurt. I set my alarm on my phone for a few minutes, and when my alarm goes off, I go and have a cup of tea, put on some music, or walk around. I make sure I change my state. I *live* on a base of foundational happiness. I *experience* everything else. And depending on the seriousness of what's happening, I decide how much time I want to spend.

In my life, I've been deeply sad. I've been deeply hurt. I've been deeply in pain and still had a choice. I deal with these respectfully. I stay with it, feel it, be there. But I also know this is a temporary state, and I can choose to do things differently and slowly start feeling things differently.

King Solomon commissioned a jeweler to make a ring that gave him joy and sadness. The jeweler engraved the ring, "This too shall pass."

However, I feel - ecstatic, really happy, on top of the world, passionate, in deep pain, sad, or disappointed I know that this too shall pass. We can forgive other people and forgive ourselves too. We choose in which emotional state we want to live. We have the power to be in a beautiful state most of the time.

I live in Pure Happiness most of the time. My beautiful state is to be happy, content, able to laugh, connect, and have great conversations. That's my way of being. That's my way of having my foundation for self-love. When I am in that state, how could I not love myself? I give myself a tap on the shoulder and say, "Good job, girl. You did it!" Living in the state of happiness I choose is an important part of my self-love.

I am mindful of how I speak to myself and ensure I don't say things to myself I would never say to someone else. I also had to stop over-evaluating things. As a presenter, we had feedback forms, especially in the Tony Robbins environment. We were rated on our performance, ability to speak clearly. Of course, I looked at the ratings!

The ratings were from zero to 10. I usually received very nice eights, nines, and 10s. A lot of 10s! Rarely, there was a six. I would fixate on that six as if it meant something was wrong with me while completely forgetting that 98% of people listed me as eight and above.

I learned rather than beat myself up or speak negatively to myself, I could see the good in the situation. I can list everything good and improve if needed. Analyzing is good, but judging, never. There is a quote that says: Thinking is difficult. That's why most people judge. Understanding myself and other people helps me be in a beautiful state to honor and respect myself and others. It allows me to have uplifting communication instead of tearing myself down.

My dad was a communicator and always said, "C'est le ton qui fait la musique" which means, "It's the tone that decides whether the music is beautiful or not".

Loving myself required very clear boundaries or standards. I decide what's okay for me and what's not, what I want, what I don't, what I tolerate, and what I won't. I communicate my boundaries because people cannot mind-read. In close relationships, I found it easiest to communicate clearly or set them together to get rid of possible arguments and make room for love.

Self-love

- Honor and respect yourself

- Be in a beautiful state

- Be aware of how you communicate to self

- Set clear boundaries

Love is a beautiful gift, especially from and to an alien with Extra ordinary Abilities!

Leveraging over 30 years working directly with business leaders in 17 countries, Connie Osterholt has synthesized her experience as a senior executive, a strategy coach, and a mentor to high-networth businesswomen in 10+ industries, public/private board members, and successful entrepreneurs. She has been consistently focused on the power of feminine and masculine energy in negotiations, networks, and the nuanced areas of business leadership.

- Author and speaker

- 25 years with Tony Robbins heading up the leadership programs.

- Speaker and facilitator of five of his core programs.

- Training and managing coaches. Platinum Partner coach, working with his top clients.

She holds a Ph.D. in psychoneurology. Her career has been based on understanding teams and individuals, looking at their behavior, personalities, and mindset in order to help them be more successful, happy, and fulfilled.

She excels at recognizing patterns that work and ones that are ready for an upgrade, training, and teaching, and making difficult concepts easily understandable.

https://www.facebook.com/connie.osterholtphd

Drconnieonline.com

https://www.linkedin.com/in/drconnieosterholt-executivecoach/

My Journey To Self-Love

By LaQuita Parks

Self-love is an amazing journey I chose to take many years ago. My journey started with a simple three-word affirmation, "I LOVE MYSELF!" I won't lie and say it was easy, but it has definitely been worth it.

The older I get, I find myself reflecting on "yesterday" more and more. Somedays, I can't help but take a trip back down the memory lane of my mind to a time when I didn't understand how important it was to love myself. I think about how my life and the entire world's lives have changed because of the pandemic. As I reflect, I quickly remind myself that while it is okay to look back over my life, it is not okay to dwell on the past... learn from it, yes, but don't dwell on it. In the last few years, I have seen more sickness, sadness, and sorrow than ever before, a constant reminder that self-love is essential.

As a victim of medical childhood trauma at the hands of a nurse, I was left crippled for life and dealing with chronic pain every day. This was what I called the beginning of my walking limitations. I knew nothing about "self-love"; as I got older, I started piling on more of those limitations. From the age of four to fourteen years old, I had surgery every year on my right leg and foot. I couldn't go outside and run and play with the other kids. I was picked out to be picked on and bullied throughout my high school years. I was the weakest link...I was a victim.

To say my self-esteem was low would be a total understatement, and loving myself was a foreign concept. I found myself trying to please people. I became more concerned with other people's mental wellness than I was with my own. I went out of my way to make sure everybody was happy. My happiness was not even a thought in my mind. I even started to believe the lies I told myself. "As long as everybody is happy, that's all that matters to me!" I said this for so long, I started to believe it!

I got tired of allowing myself to be treated as though I was not as important as anyone else. I got tired of being disregarded and treated like a victim. One morning, I took a long hard look at myself in the mirror and said, "Today is going to be a great day because I am going to make it so!" And guess what? It was a great day. That was when I discovered the power of affirmations.

I started studying the bible and understanding what love and true sacrifice really were. I began to read self-help books and listen to inspirational and motivational messages. My "mirror" conversations became opportunities for me to experiment. Every morning, I would make up an affirmation that I would repeat throughout the day. "I Love Myself" was and is still my favorite. I began to notice my confidence grew, my self-esteem increased, and I no longer felt like I was the "weakest link!" To encourage others, I even wrote and published a book of motivation and inspiration called "Good Morning Friends." (Available on Amazon)

Everything I do begins with a thought, whether good, bad, or ugly...a thought about it has to occur. If I think I can't, then I won't, but if I think I can, I certainly will. Affirmation is the action or process of affirming something. Simply put, it is the act of repeating a positive statement until positive changes occur. These changes can be in the form of dreams realized, goals achieved or mindsets changed from negative to positive. But the key to allowing affirmations was to reshape my thinking with "repetition." My "I Love Myself" affirmations set a new course for my life.

My journey on the road to "self-love" has seen its share of bitter and sweet. Admittingly, some days were really good while some were really bad but when I started being intentional with my own self-talk and staying committed on the road to loving myself as much as I loved others, my life changed.

Below are some tips I used to remind myself that I matter and that loving myself is not selfish but necessary.

Tips on "How to Love Yourself!"

Make a List of Things You Like About Yourself!

Take a few moments each day and remind yourself of the positives and your good qualities. This is the opportunity I take to "toot" my own horn. Do not be shy. Make a list of all the good, and add to it as often as possible.

Treat Yourself Like a Best Friend!

Challenge yourself daily to achieve your best life possible. Love and support yourself, treat yourself with kindness and respect just like you would your closest friend. When I started treating myself as my best friend, I learned to love ME more.

Pay Attention to Your Needs and Desires!

"What do YOU want?" One of the best ways to love yourself is simply to pay attention to what it is that you want and need. I really had to work on this one because I was too busy meeting other peoples' needs and desires that I never took the time to consider my own.

Protect Yourself!

Protect yourself from people who don't have your best interest at heart. Choose not to allow yourself to be treated unlovingly and disrespectfully. Recognize the signs. Someone once told me those flags (warning signs) are not saying Go! Loving yourself means not taking chances on your safety.

Listen to Your Self-Talk!

Commit to making your self-talk positive. As you talk to yourself, don't say anything you wouldn't say to someone else you love. Say "I Love Myself" every day. Show yourself compassion and be willing to forgive yourself for mistakes. Be patient as you grow.

Take Care of Your Body!

Do your best to be healthy. Exercise and eat "good" food! Treating our bodies well sends a strong message of self-love. We can't expect to put junk into our bodies, minds, and souls and think we will feel good. Self-love means taking care of the whole you. If one thing is out of whack, everything is out of whack.

Take Care of Your Inner Life!

Don't neglect your spirit. Slow down long enough to pay attention to what's going on with you. Self-love also means taking the time to pray, meditate, and study the bible. This helps nourish my love for myself and enrich the lives of others.

Prepare for Your Future BUT Live in the Now

One powerful way to love yourself is to focus your energy and attention on the present moment. Don't dwell on the past, even when painful regrets live there. Make a self-investment in appreciating all the good in your life right now. Make the most of who you are RIGHT NOW!

Remember that loving yourself isn't selfish. To truly understand someone else, you have to take time to get to know them. To truly understand yourself, you have to take just as much time to get to know YOU! When we don't understand the true meaning of love and how important it is to love ourselves FIRST, we continue to expect our happiness to come from other people, and we will be constantly walking in the limitations they set for us. This is a lesson that has taken me a long time to learn but I get it now. In order to love someone else or even recognize someone else's love, I have to first love myself. The more loving I am to myself, the more love I will be able to send out to the other people in my life.

Love is not a feeling, it's a decision. Make a choice right now to love yourself and to work on loving yourself more...from the inside out!

The first step in loving yourself is to START!

Set Goals

Think positively!

Accept responsibility for your thoughts, feelings, and actions!

Re-train your thinks (how you see things)

168

Take small steps (one at a time)

I started my journey of self love. I learned to embrace the journey and understand it is ongoing. My self-love goals continue, one small step at a time.

LaQuita is the Founder and CEO of Pa-Pro-Vi Publishing Company and A Failure 2 Communicate LLC as well as a Relationship Communication Coach, Writing Coach and Mentor with a passion for people and their well-being. She is also the host of her own podcast show, "My Heart on Pages" and the host of "The Power of YOUR Story" radio show. LaQuita is also the Founder and Facilitator of EXHALE-a social communication group for women who meet to discuss different issues, ranging from personal to political.

LaQuita created the Pa-Pro-Vi Publishing platform to help people start the healing process because she believes that there is power in YOUR story and that writing and sharing your story can be therapeutic. Walking Limitations is LaQuita's first published book and the true story of how she went into the hospital to have a simple procedure and it left her crippled for life at the hands of a nurse. This created a medical tsunami that has affected her life for the last forty-nine years. Writing her story started the healing process for her and she helps others do the same with their story. Since starting Pa-Pro-Vi Publishing in 2020, LaQuita has been able to help clients all over the country take their stories from a "thought to a realization." LaQuita coaches' people through the process of how to start writing their stories. What makes LaQuita successful is the fact that she is not only a listener, but she is compassionate and has a genuine love and passion for people.

In 2022, LaQuita received the T.R.I.V.I.A. Inspirational Radio's Community Excellence Award and was named Woman of the Year by Making Headline News. Not only is LaQuita a self-published author of several books including her semi autobiography titled Walking Limitations, and two popular children's books called "My Neighbors Don't Look Like Me", and "Ouch Lies Hurt", she is also a contributing writer and sponsor for I Am International Magazine and has been featured on the Zondra TV Network and numerous TV, radio and podcast platforms.

LaQuita is a Christian and a single mother of three adult children ages 28, 31 and 33 and has 5 little heartbeats that call her Nanna.

LaQuita lives in a small town outside of Atlanta, Georgia.

Connect with me through all my platforms

LaQuita Parks CEO/Founder of Pa-Pro-Vi Publishing

678-608-9948

https://paprovipublishing.com/

https://www.facebook.com/laquita.parks.3

https://www.linkedin.com/in/laquita-parks-a03647a/

https://twitter.com/AFTC_LaQuita

https://www.instagram.com/paprovipublishing/

https://www.youtube.com/channel/UCK5HfhwZ8XtCaT
sdmNReLVQ

Haydens Way, Statistically Speaking

By Mistilei Wriston

Two cents is not a lot of money. Nowadays, if I saw two pennies, I would pick them up, bring them home, toss them in a baggie of water, and tack them to the wall to keep flies out of the chicken coop.

Giving someone my two cents is to give my opinion, which often, or at least occasionally, has value, especially for myself. This is where it starts to get exciting. I noticed the value of the smallest conversations and moments between "the right" two people to be priceless. The value of a momentary rainbow in the sky or a hummingbird landing right next to me, tiny, happy moments like these: priceless. The value of listening to my daily spoken words: unbelievably priceless. I see the messages are always for me. Capturing these words and things on paper daily is how I built a superpower.

My mind has since worked with the idea that the tiniest overlap with another human, plant, animal, or moment could create the most significant changes in my life, good or bad, powerfully expansive or equally devastating. My brain wanted to know more about the why. Why could a tiny thing, something someone said, or an interaction change one person for the better and destroy another? Finding and staying aligned with the positive outcomes became a theme for my mission in life.

I paid attention when I heard statistics of mass failure. After my son's very complicated delivery, a woman who should not have spoken to me at all, casually mentioned, "It is so sad when a child is born like yours. The parents usually end up divorced."

I have forgotten much about the tragic and tumultuous day my son was born, yet I remember that statement clearly. She was out of line, and she was right. The statistics were dismal.

It triggered/reminded me of a time at age 13 when I read something that said that less than 5% of people would stop generational trauma and abuse. My life was filled with abuse in many ways. One thing I knew for sure; I would not continue my family's behavior. I would be the tiny percent that made a different choice and made the change. If it was possible, then it was possible for me!

That woman's "two-bit" comment in the hospital changed me. I became obsessed with beating the odds. In my case, divorce was inevitable; however, the other statistics for a single mother of four children, one with intense special needs, were horrific to consider. I went from a career path on the Concord, flying internationally to get rid of corporate waste, to what seemed destined to be a complete dependency on the welfare system of Texas. I knew I could not continue to live this life unless I made massive, statistically unlikely changes.

I eventually left the state to clear my husband's reach and walked away from my helpless stepdaughters despite their difficult parenting situation. My children and I spent a short time sleeping in the van, and I began a lifelong journey of keeping myself out of the statistics.

I wanted to love my children, feed them clean food, and keep them out of jail and babies out of the equation until they were grown. Ideally, all without destroying them in the process since I had a lot of things in the self-love folder that were actually abuse. I unknowingly explored many attractive addictions; some even gave out awards.

I needed to work harder and longer than everyone else. I would not be the welfare statistic. I knew if we were to survive, it was up to me. Three jobs at once, then down to only two to one to one of my very own, I climbed out of that welfare trap. I beat those odds. My son Hayden Ray was there along the way, teaching me his ways- Never give up and stick with what works.

I won awards and made plenty of money while three of my children raised themselves, and they or the nurse cared for Hayden. I made baby steps that seemed huge and hurt like hell. I quit drinking and smoking; my former entertainment veiled under the Self-love category. I would not be a statistic.

Sobriety provided clarity. My self-love game took a hard-core U-turn. I realized I needed more two-cent conversations and activities and had to cut out the two-bit kind right along with the alcohol. Again, the odds were not in my favor. So, I went cold turkey with no excuses. It was brutal and efficient. I could probably drink again. I don't think I could survive another 'get sober.' Once was enough and ensured I would not be part of those statistics.

When I wasn't working, I felt compelled to share the magic of sobriety with everyone, even those that didn't ask. Sober seemed hard and kind of boring. I wanted more people on my team. No one wanted to join. I could not give my two cents away. This seemed to be a pattern of mine as I looked back. I habitually wanted to "help " others who had not asked rather than looking at my own world.

I had to write a new story. Work was a long-time friend and welcomed me back as many hours as I would grind. It became painfully apparent that I needed to be home more when my 15-year-old and $100,000 sports car sailed through the air with ease at 165 mph. The wake-up call was real. He recovered physically completely while I completely came unraveled.

I was personally miserable and happily sober and lived a postcard life until I got home, nice and early, for this mythical "family time." Life was so complicated and confusing. I knew it was time to align...again. I had no idea how I would do this, but I knew the journey only gets clearer as I removed those items that didn't serve me or clouded my vision.

I had seen it with every major change and course correction. My obvious next steps were to continue loving myself, being home, spending time with my children, and loving my body. A doctor told me statistically, my current lifestyle and lack of sleep would kill me, and I probably would not even stop to call 911. It was time to get back to Hayden's Way. Never give up, and stick to what works. Write the story I do want.

I went on a deep dive into personal development and followed the advice to the letter. I lost 75 pounds and made even more money. I had time to travel a bit with one of the groups, and in every event, I learned more from the access I had to the crowd than from the speaker I paid to attend. There were people with shiny, happy, say Yes, Two-

Cent thoughts all around and accessible to me. They were becoming my people.

I FINALLY realized I was choosing to hang out in two-bit conversations while pretending that my "kind of people" didn't exist or were hard to find. It turned out Two Cent people were everywhere. I traveled to eight countries in one year, and these shiny two-cent humans were at each location. It took me a while to remember that I already knew how I succeeded. Watch those that have what I want. Watch what they do that I don't. Do those things.

While reading my journals from the weeks and months after I quit drinking, I saw how my emotions flowed, how my friends changed, and how many things became apparent about how I treated myself. Not everything could fit through the funnel with me to MY next level, nor did they all want to. It was clearly written in my journal, in my handwriting. NOT EVERYONE GETS TO GO WITH YOU ON YOUR NEXT PAGE. NOT EVERYONE WANTS TO.

I wrote words just like this after a long overdue divorce. I wrote this after my weight loss passed 100 pounds, and I was no longer the fat friend. The pain was temporary, even when very painful, as long as I focused on my goal. Same story, written over and over just before I met my goal. This was a stat I could support. I have survived 100% of my days so far.

I flipped back to my journal from twenty years prior, when I opened my company twenty years earlier. Times were hard, and I had the choice to fail or progress. My district manager gave me a mirror for my desk. "If it is going to be, it's up to me." I could change the story. The lessons and emotions, and steps were the same. I only had to read my journals to clearly see what had worked, what hadn't, and what stories I love to use repetitively to explain when things don't go my way. It was FASCINATING.

I discovered my blatant co-dependency by comparing old journals. I learned as much from the lies I wrote myself in my journal when I decided a day was bad or a partner did me wrong in some way as I did when I clearly detailed the steps I took to succeed. It was my own riddle, and I solved it. For a moment, I wanted to be frustrated that I had not learned this sooner and kept even more of my journals. Luckily, I realized today was as good a day as any to start taking this seriously. With my knowledge and Hayden's Way of looking at things, I was unstoppable.

I sold almost everything to take advantage of the housing market boom. I sold my oversized family home now that all but one had moved out. Hayden and I moved into our RV (with my art supplies, journals, notebooks, plants, chickens, and dogs) and spent the next two years, almost to the day, exploring the lakes and mountains and breathtaking scenery while avoiding the germs. We lived completely unplugged and off-grid for a while and eventually landed in our beautiful home in Western Arkansas. When I say I am paraphrasing our adventures, this is a gross understatement.

There were many struggles along the way. Each time I felt that heavy feeling of overwhelm, I would return to one of my old journals. I could easily mark out the current What and Who and see the pattern and How I got out of it the last time I slipped into a pattern where self-love took a backseat. When I stepped out of my alignment, my journals had the answers. LIFE BECAME CLEARER when I followed the steps to get back in alignment—100% of the time.

I began to write more diligently and with brutal honesty. I also spent equal time writing a future I DID want without mentioning my ails and troubles. Alone in the mountains with my non-verbal sidekick, I learned to use our future for my entertainment and then as my power. My stories became my favorite show to binge. I could use my real life to create situations and have them end precisely how I wanted on paper. I could read my notes for old patterns that limited me and signs of my success. I became very aware of the moment when I realized I could not even think of the desired outcome. Those moments when I used to feel there was no hope became the doorway to unlimited hope and possibilities. Hayden showed me there is always a way, even when I didn't know it.

The more I wrote the "fairy tale," the easier it was to make slight changes to stay aligned. I didn't experience confusion when truly in alignment, genuinely caring for myself, and honestly practicing self-love. When I came to a scenario I could not imagine, rather than feeling hopeless and overwhelmed, I learned to see it as an opportunity to create, outside my imagination, using my secrets to success.

The more I held myself to this pattern, the more others noticed. I sold my former corporate business and found work I love in words. I changed how I treated myself in every way and attracted more people I could be around while treating myself with absolute self-love. As I felt the wounds of people I loved falling away when my ways no longer fit theirs, or theirs mine, I found solace in my journals. I knew this meant new energy was on the way as long as I stayed ready to receive. My profession began to morph into my playtime. My passion and purpose were playful and peaceful.

Some changes hurt worse than others. My son, my best friend, and a child that stayed a newborn, my newborn for 28 years, Hayden Ray, passed away last month. This one hurt more than all other losses combined. The steps to continue, survive and thrive are higher, deeper, and harder to climb; however, they are the same. I can prepare and sit with these emotions. They are no longer a surprise, even when I want my situation to be somehow different or more hopeless than anyone else's. Hayden had already shown me the way.

When he was born, my world was very empty. My son became the audience to all of my stories, the comedies, the love stories, the tragedies, and the strategies. He has never spoken since birth, so I also imagined his lines. I decided long ago my son would have been hysterical had he been born with the ability to speak. His side helped hold me accountable. Caring for him held me accountable.

On June 2, 2023, Hayden Ray passed away and quite literally put me in charge of my story. Since he passed, I have read many of my older journals. I have watched hours of my own content on grief and pain. I began following the steps the first morning I woke up without him. It was so painfully and beautifully clear; the path to self-love will be exactly the same, only the pace will be different.

Write the story I DO want.

Find the bliss.

Feel the gratitude.

Stay ready to receive the blessings.

Remove everything that is not serving me and the desired future.

Stay in alignment.

Keep writing.

Repeat.

This method has worked for me with 100% effectiveness in every situation I have applied it. I've now lost 130 pounds using Hayden's Way. I have stayed sober and tobacco-free for over nine years using Hayden's Way. I changed every aspect of my life until I found a way to live in bliss, even when experiencing pain, and helped hundreds do the same. It was always Hayden's Way.

I am at the beginning of a new journey. I am on chapter one of applying Hayden's Way to maneuver my grief journey. I was his caregiver for just over half of my life. Every decision I have made has been around his needs. Writing the first line of the first story without my son in it was the hardest thing I have ever put on paper. I did it because I will be part of one statistic, the small percent who choose to thrive even when...

I have seen humans go through this and thrive. I have also seen this destroy people. That means I CAN do this if I choose to. Thankfully, I have my secret to success, and I allow myself to listen to the wisdom of my self-love recipe, even when... Hayden's Way is the way to self-love.

Write the story I DO want.

Find the bliss.

Feel the gratitude.

Stay ready to receive the blessings.

Remove everything that is not serving me and the desired future.

Stay in alignment.

Keep writing.

Repeat.

It works! Statistically speaking.

Mistilei went from Financial CEO to a Fabulously Feral lifestyle. She is a conversational healer, multiple #1

181

International Best Selling Author, TV host, speaker, content creator, publisher, compiler, animal and outdoor lover, and master of Alignment, and this list changes daily. Mistilei is dedicated to showing others how to work with grief, pain, and addictions to ride the waves, ending the sink-or-swim cycle. Schedule a stay onsite in Western Arkansas at one of our retreats, or host your own at our Paradise in the Ouachita Mountains.

https://www.facebook.com/MistiWriston
https://calendly.com/campgroundtbd/goals

https://www.facebook.com/groups/quantumwriting300

campgroundtbd@gmail.com

Hayden's Ray 501(c)(3), Grief Relief Space and Sobriety Prehab.

Self-Love: My Life Changing Commitment to Happiness and Fulfillment

By Steve Thomas

As I sit here, thinking about my life's journey, I see that one of the concepts that most deeply impacted me is the practice of self-love. It's an ongoing process that demands patience, acceptance, and a steadfast commitment to nurturing my well-being. Every step toward embracing self-love uncovers new layers of authenticity and inner peace.

Self-love begins with acceptance. I've learned to embrace some of my flaws, imperfections, and insecurities without passing judgment. I recognize that I am a work in progress. Through my challenges, I can grow and evolve. Instead of criticizing myself for my mistakes or dwelling on past failures, I forgive and show compassion. This self-forgiveness has liberated me from the chains of self-criticism and allowed me to develop a more loving relationship with myself.

At times, I catch myself comparing my journey to that of others. However, I now understand that comparison steals away our joy. I've learned to celebrate my unique qualities and accomplishments without measuring them against others. This change in perspective has allowed me to appreciate my individuality and value my self-worth.

Nurturing self-love also entails prioritizing self-care. I've learned that taking care of my physical, emotional, and mental well-being is not a vain or selfish act but rather an essential one. By prioritizing my needs and setting boundaries, I've been able to preserve my energy and avoid burnout. Whether indulging in a relaxing bath, engaging in creative pursuits, or simply taking a moment to breathe, self-care has become an integral part of my daily routine.

Self-love extends beyond the physical realm as well. It involves nourishing my mind and spirit. I've discovered the power of positive affirmations, which gently remind me of my inherent worth and capabilities. I've witnessed a profound transformation in how I perceive myself by consciously shifting my inner dialogue from self-criticism to self-encouragement. The love and kindness I show myself in my thoughts reflect in my actions and relationships with others.

Self-love has taught me the importance of establishing healthy boundaries. It's not just about preserving my well-being but also about respecting my needs and desires. By saying "no" when necessary and asserting myself gently yet firmly, I've learned to create space for my growth and happiness. Boundaries enable me to prioritize my time and energy, ensuring I am fully present and engaged in activities and relationships that bring me joy and fulfillment.

In pursuing self-love, I've realized that forgiveness is integral to the process. Holding onto grudges and resentment only weighs me down, hindering my ability to move forward. By choosing to forgive myself and others, I liberate myself from the burden of negativity and make room for healing and growth. Forgiveness is not a sign of weakness; instead, a testament to my strength and resilience.

As I carry on this self-love journey, I've discovered that it's not a destination but a lifelong commitment. It requires continuous introspection, self-reflection, and a willingness to let go of old patterns and beliefs that no longer serve me. I've learned to trust, listen to my intuition, and honor my needs. Through self-love, I have unlocked the power to live authentically and joyfully.

Self-love is a profound and transformative experience that empowers me to embrace my authenticity and worthiness. It is an ongoing journey of acceptance, forgiveness, and self-care. I have discovered an unshakeable foundation of inner peace and contentment by nurturing self-love. I am grateful for this journey and its beautiful transformation in my life.

I love myself. I love my flaws, my quirks, and my imperfections. I love my body, my mind, and my soul. I love the way I make others feel, and I love the way I make myself feel. I am worthy of love, and I am deserving of happiness.

I have come a long way in my journey to self-love. There was a time when I despised myself. I believed I was unattractive, unintelligent, and worthless. I did drugs, drank too much, and stayed up too late. I ate wrong, didn't drink enough of the right fluids, and smoked cigarettes. I thought I could never measure up and doubted anyone could love me.

Then, I started to change my thinking. I began to focus on my positive qualities and appreciate myself for who I am. I learned to love myself unconditionally and realized I deserve all the good things in life.

If you struggle with self-love, I encourage you to start your journey. It is not easy, but it is worth it. Here are a few tips that helped me on my journey:

- I was kind to myself.

- I forgave myself for my mistakes and focused on my strengths.

- I practiced positive self-talk, telling myself I was attractive, intelligent, and capable. I got my GED, wrote a chapter in the anthology, Now What, and other self-affirming things.

- I surrounded myself with positive people who loved and supported me, and they helped me recognize my worth. It is truly amazing to me how important it is to get around positive, forward-looking people. The times that have been hardest for me were when I'd been surrounded by people that were vibrating at lower frequencies, always angry or depressed.

- I engaged in activities that brought me joy, spending time with loved ones, pursuing my passions, and caring for my physical and mental health.

- I gave back to others, knowing that helping them made me feel good about myself and positively impacted the world.

Self-love is an essential aspect of a healthy and fulfilling life. For me, self-love involves taking care of myself both physically and mentally. This means nourishing my body with nutritious food, exercising regularly, getting enough restful sleep, and practicing mindfulness and meditation to cultivate a positive mindset.

In today's society, self-love seems to be a popular term frequently discussed. However, its true meaning is often misconstrued. Self-love means accepting oneself, including all strengths and weaknesses, and treating oneself with kindness and respect. It means recognizing our own worth and making our well-being a priority while also acknowledging our limitations.

Self-love plays a crucial role in personal development and growth. It involves embracing and appreciating who we are, both in terms of our positive qualities and areas for improvement. Practicing self-love can be challenging in a fast-paced world that often encourages self-criticism. That's why taking small daily steps toward cultivating self-love is essential.

Self-love is an aspect of our lives that is often overlooked but is tremendously important. It requires us to acknowledge our inherent value and prioritize our own needs. Practicing self-love can sometimes feel selfish in a world that often emphasizes putting others first. However, it is vital for our mental and emotional well-being.

Self-love is essential for individual well-being and plays a significant role in the success of my marriage. By practicing self-love, I can bring my best self into the relationship, establish healthy boundaries, communicate effectively, and foster a supportive and nurturing partnership. Embracing self-love allows my wife and I to grow individually and together, creating a solid foundation for a fulfilling and lasting relationship. Here are some insights on how self-love contributes to our partnership:

- Enhanced Emotional Well-being: When we practice self-love, we develop a deeper understanding and acceptance of ourselves. This self-awareness allows us to be more emotionally available and stable in our relationship. I can approach my partner with love, empathy, and support by nurturing my emotional well-being.

- Building Strong Boundaries: Self-love helps individuals establish and maintain healthy boundaries in their relationships. We can better identify and communicate our needs effectively and ensure they are met. By respecting and valuing ourselves, we create an environment that encourages mutual respect and fosters a sense of safety and trust within the partnership.

- Improved Communication: Self-love enables individuals to have healthier relationships with their thoughts and emotions. This self-awareness and emotional intelligence translate into better communication skills within the relationship. When individuals have a strong foundation of self-love, we can express our needs, desires, and concerns more effectively, and we are also more open to actively listening to each other.

- Increased Resilience: Self-love allows individuals to cultivate a strong sense of self-worth and confidence. When faced with challenges or conflicts in the relationship, individuals who practice self-love are better equipped to navigate them constructively. They can bounce back from setbacks, take responsibility for their actions, and work towards resolutions that benefit both partners.

- Balanced Partnership: Self-love encourages us to prioritize well-being, crucial for maintaining a balanced and fulfilling partnership. We bring our best selves into the relationship by caring for ourselves physically, emotionally, and mentally. This self-care not only benefits them but also contributes to the overall health and happiness of the partnership.

- Empathy and Understanding: Practicing self-love fosters empathy and understanding, which translates into empathy and understanding towards my partner. When I am compassionate towards my flaws and imperfections, I am more likely to extend the same compassion and understanding to my wife. This creates a nurturing environment where both of us feel accepted and supported.

- Avoiding Codependency: Self-love prevents the pitfalls of co-dependency, where we rely on each other for validation, happiness, and a sense of self-worth. When we have a strong foundation of self-love, we can maintain our independence and pursue our individual growth and interests. This healthy autonomy contributes to the growth and longevity of the relationship.

- Role Modeling: When we both practice self-love, we become positive role models for each other and potentially our kids. By demonstrating self-acceptance, self-care, and healthy boundaries, we increase the chances they create a loving and respectful environment that encourages personal growth and self-love within their partnerships.

I am incredibly grateful that I discovered self-love. It has transformed my life for the better. I am happier, healthier, and more confident than ever before. I am a better husband and father. I am living a much better life and know you can too.

If you struggle with self-love, please know you are not alone. Many people have been through similar experiences. You can overcome this. You are worthy of love and happiness. Self-love is a journey, not a destination. It is something that requires daily effort. But it *is* worth it. You become happier, healthier, and more successful when you love yourself.

You live *your* best life.

Steve Thomas is an author, entrepreneur, coach, and co-creator of Quantum Writing 300.

He has dedicated over a decade to personal development and self-improvement. Steve has helped thousands of individuals unleash their potential and achieve their goals.

As an entrepreneur, Steve's focus is now on longevity, stem cells, and helping others live pain-free, body, mind, and soul.

Through coaching, writing, and speaking, he inspires and empowers people to take charge of their lives and reach their full potential.

He and his wife live in Oklahoma, where they coach, garden, and continually seek new ways to achieve freedom!

He can be found at https://www.facebook.com/stevethomas6177, but he would rather you look for him in #QW300 community!

https://www.facebook.com/groups/quantumwriting300

Self Love - A Journey & A Practice

By Jonathan Troen

I used to look in the mirror, cringing at the details of my face and hair. I would recount my day and recall all the blunders and mistakes that I made to the point of insanity. I required constant sound, music, television, anything other than silence. Silence was too hard to take. The voices were just too loud.

I lived in Santa Monica, California, one of the most beautiful places on the planet. I worked in Hollywood, the land of dreams, interviewing the biggest stars. But inside my brain, the stories of inadequacy kept going. It didn't matter how successful I was. I could not be good enough for myself.

This was my life, and I wondered how long it would last.

I was completely focused on Outer Wealth - just as I had been taught: money in the bank, the car, the romantic relationships, and what other people thought of me. But none of that made me happy. So I left the entertainment business and went on a journey to figure out what was wrong with me. I soon found out that I wasn't alone. Some of the wealthiest people on the planet were unhappy. My world was turned upside down. Everything I understood about success was apparently wrong.

After studying many different teachers and researching different techniques and strategies, I made the most significant discovery of my life. **I discovered this: nothing was wrong with me!**

192

I came across the most important missing ingredient of life and success. It was called Self Love. No one ever spoke about it to me when I was growing up, and it wasn't in any of the books assigned to me in high school or college.

The first time I saw Louise Hay talk about it on YouTube, her idea seemed interesting. She said to look yourself in the mirror and say, "I love you."

I thought that sounded fun! I stood up from the computer, walked to my bathroom, and looked at my face in the mirror. I tried to speak the words, but they wouldn't come. My voice was paralyzed. This odd sensation overtook me, and I curled up in a ball on the floor.

It felt like a truck had hit me.

If you asked me moments earlier if I love myself, I would have emphatically said yes. But in that moment, I know something was wrong.

I didn't give up though. I researched. I practiced. I researched more and practiced more. And after a few years of practice, things started to make sense. I discovered that I was the only one who was holding me back, making me feel the way I was. And that by just being kind to myself, and accepting myself as I am - the wonderful and the not-so-wonderful - that life could become truly joyous.

That was a huge awakening for me. But once I realized it, everything began to change.

I had spent my life trying not to be me, but to be like the more successful or popular people. I was trying to be anyone but me. And now, for the first time, I stopped trying to be someone else.

Being myself was odd at first. I had to wake up a different part of my brain. The muscle was weak, but over time this muscle strengthened. Over time, I realized I was perfect just the way I was.

Now here's the really crazy part: Once I accepted myself as I was, I began to change for the better. I started to help more people and became more confident in my ability to help them. It created an upward spiral. Instead of wondering how much longer life would last, I wondered how many people I could help today.

I had been trying to change myself and everything around me, and it was not working. So I had to try something different. I threw away all the success strategies my teachers and family taught me and invited a new paradigm into my life.

Of course, Self Love on its own wasn't enough. I couldn't even say the words to myself at first. Self Love was the goal, but it didn't exist on its own, at least not for me.

I built my home of self-love with four components—first, the Foundation.

The Foundation was Complete Acceptance. Before we change things, we must accept them as they are. It's a great paradox in life that lasting change really occurs only once we have accepted things as they are.

I had to accept my starting point, which is always right here and now. At first, this acceptance thing didn't work for me. I didn't like what was happening right here and right now. How could I accept something I didn't like?

This is where Complete Acceptance came in. I had to accept what was and the fact that I wanted it to be different.

Not only was it ok that I wanted it to be different, but it was also a necessary part of acceptance to accept that I wanted it to be different. Now the door to freedom began to open.

Everything before that made me feel like I was wrong. I couldn't change my thoughts, so I was wrong. I couldn't accept things, so I was wrong. This made everything right. I had to accept what was happening because it was, in fact, happening. And now I had permission to want it to be different.

Next is gratitude. I could not practice Self Love until I became truly grateful, the first wall in my Self-Love Home. It was much more than writing in my journal every night. Gratitude became an experience I felt in my body.

Gratitude is much more than writing in your journal every night. I remember one client I was working with. Shortly after we started working together, I asked him about his gratitude practice. He proudly said he writes in his gratitude journal every night. Excited, I asked, "And how do you feel afterward?" He answered, "Nothing. I just get it done and then move to the next thing." It became simply an item on his checklist that he needed to do.

Gratitude is more than an item on a to-do list. Gratitude is an experience. Gratitude must be felt in the body. If you don't feel it in your body, you're not practicing gratitude.

When we experience gratitude, the body releases dopamine and serotonin, sometimes called the happiness hormones. Dopamine is the big reward hormone. It's what you get when scrolling through Facebook or checking your email. Your compulsion to check is simply the body asking for a shot of dopamine. So you could check your email or scroll social media for the next hour, or you can simply experience gratitude. You will get your dopamine hit and can get back to work.

The next supporting wall was Forgiveness. Without forgiveness, I found Self Love impossible. Even with gratitude, I could not practice Self Love without forgiveness.

I call Forgiveness is the most important skill we have never been taught. There three paths of forgiveness:

1. Forgiveness of others

2. Asking for forgiveness from others

3. Forgiveness of yourself (the most difficult for myself and many others).

The thing about Forgiveness is that it's a skill. The more we practice it the better we become at it. And when we get good at it, it's one of the most powerful skills we have. Without forgiveness, we live in the past - wishing for a different past. Living in the past prevented me from creating a new future and feeling free.

"Forgiveness is giving up hope that the past can be different." -Dr. Gerald Jampolsky

The past can't be different. And thinking about how life would be different if only that one thing didn't happen doesn't make life different. Instead, it takes energy away from living today, and creating the life that I, and you, want to live.

Replaying the past in my head was a trap I had been stuck in for years. Forgiveness is a secret key that opens the trap door to let you out. Practicing forgiveness offers ultimate freedom.

I began a practice of saying this every night before bed:

Bedtime Forgiveness Ritual

I forgive myself and all who may have hurt or offended

me physically, monetarily, or emotionally. Whether

knowingly or unknowingly. I wish them no harm. I accept

this moment. And I release myself from any future pain.

I invite you to say this every night before bed for the next 30 days. And then ask yourself, Do you sleep better? Are your days better? Is this a practice you want to continue?

197

My last support wall is words of Self Compassion, saying kind things to me about myself. When I couldn't say, "I love you" to myself, I found I could complement my eyes and smile. I could thank my neck for turning, my ears for hearing, and my knees for getting me up the stairs. I could also celebrate my accomplishments of the day, big and small.

I make mistakes every day. I acknowledge the mistakes (Complete Acceptance) to see if there's any learning I can take from them. Then, I spend the majority of my time celebrating the successes, big or small. I found so much to celebrate when I looked for it. I trained my mind to look for the good. Peace and joy became my best friends.

With the foundation and the walls in place, we can now cover the house with the Roof of Self Love. A roof that offers us safety from the chaos that we call life. Notice, I do not have a 4th wall - there are only three. The house of Self Love is always open. We don't need to build extra walls and fences in a world of Self Love. We can simply open ourselves to the beauty the world wants to send our way, the uplifting miracles as well as the painful moments. We can welcome them all - they are all a part of a beautiful life. This open home of self love helps us create deeper and loving connections, with ourselves and others. And it's these deep, loving connections that allow us to feel free, and they are the reason we are here, together, on this planet.

Jonathan Troen is a Self Love Mentor, Life Mastery Coach, and creator of the Self Love Revolution. He is also the co-founder of the Austin-based mindfulness center, Austin Yoga Tree.

Jonathan's mission: To help people find the joy in side of themselves.

Jonathan spent 20+ years in the entertainment industry. He was living the life of his dreams, meeting the biggest stars in the world, except he wasn't happy. And he couldn't figure out why. He began studying people: how they live, what motivated them, and how they defined success. His studies brought him to one conclusion: Most of us are mean to ourselves, and all we really want is to be loved. He also discovered that when we seek love from outside of ourselves, it is fleeting. Lasting love comes from inside of us. And since we're not taught to love ourselves, this creates a problem.

Jonathan created the Self Love Revolution specifically to share the methodology he created after 15 years of research and practice.

Jonathan's belief: We all deserve success. We all deserve to be loved. And we all deserve to be treated kindly, especially by ourselves.

Jonathan has been featured locally on ABC Austin, CBS Austin, Fox 7 Austin, NBC Tampa Bay and has been a featured speaker at SXSW with his signature talk, Self Love Revolution: The New Pathway to Success.

Website: https://www.SelfLoveRevolution.com
Facebook: https://www.facebook.com/jonathantroen
Instagram: https://www.instagram.com/jonathantroen/
LinkedIn: https://www.linkedin.com/in/troen/
YouTube: https://SelfLoveRevolution.com/youtube
Apple Podcast: https://SelfLoveRevolution.com/podcast

Permission Granted

By Douglas Jessup

Is there a baby elephant in the room? Although truly free, are you still living where you are simply to appease family or because you FEEL stuck? Maybe, just maybe, it's time for you to MAKE A CHANGE. Look UP and look AROUND! Take charge of your future and recognize that you are allowed to move your life ANYWHERE! Reboot, refresh, and start anew!

10,000 Baby Boomers retire daily, and this will continue for the next twenty years. Some will retire at 50 and some at 70, but eventually, most will retire because they can. We are, after all, the first generation that have a 401K, stock options, and significant home equity. As a result, we may be able to retire with the same lifestyle that our earning years provided, in fact, for some even better.

We now have choices and don't have to stay where we landed. People are moving away from where they were born more than ever before. In our transit society, most of us went to a couple of different elementary schools and went off to college, never to return to our "hometown'.

We are the first generation with the freedom to move to senior-friendly locations at retirement. For the first 150 years of American history, people lived out their entire lives where they were born. My grandparents, Homer and Mable Jessup (two of my favorite old people names), were born, raised, and lived until they died in Hancock County, Indiana. They never lived more than two miles away from their birthplace. This was also true for my aunts, uncles, and cousins. They consider themselves

HOOSIERS from the cradle to the grave. They enjoyed the stability and significant social support this provides. It wasn't until the rebellion of the sixties that adults realized they could give themselves the freedom to move away.

Droves of people headed to big cities in pursuit of better-paying jobs. Many of these folks retired and moved to Arizona or Florida. For decades, these two states offered the best combination of warmer winters and tax breaks for those with the courage and the resources. Added to the senior discounts offered at Shoney's Big Boy and Denny's, you find where most retired folk headed if they had the financial freedom to do so.

My grandma on my mother's side, Evelyn was one of them. She married for the third time late in life. After losing two husbands, she met the true love of her life, John McCarthy. They decided to leave the Hoosier state and travel the country in a fifth wheel. Like many their age, they kept a place to call home in Sun City, Arizona, known to many as GREY HAIR CENTRAL, near Phoenix. This was a seniors-only trailer park where something was happening every night of the week; card games or a book discussion at the clubhouse, shuffleboard and horseshoes at the park, water aerobics in the pool, dances, and big parties on holidays. Never a dull moment for the active senior. While in her eighties, my grandmother was all about fun and loved every minute of living in Arizona. She always commented how great she felt in the "dry heat". She was a great example to me of one who had the courage, although late in life, to follow her heart.

We now live with a different mindset. For the first time in U.S. history, Americans are considering other options beyond Arizona and Florida. Many have vacationed in Europe, studied abroad, and even worked in other countries. Now that we are getting older, we are the first generation looking at INTERNATIONAL options. My research tells me that although 50% are choosing to retire and stay where they made a living, the other 50% are moving to a place that suits them better. They have the freedom to live where they have always dreamed of living. Roughly 25% are considering moving abroad, with Costa Rica, Belize, Portugal, Panama, Dominican Republic, **Mexico**, and Italy at the top of the location lists.

I made a "GRID" of the most important things my perfect senior's living location must have. Then, after laying it out, and looking at each possibility under a thoughtful microscope, I visited three that made the cut, and it became clear to me. For me, it was CABO.

I heard stories of plans to retire without first going there in person. Big mistake! Others made their choice as a result of a cruise stop or short vacation visit. Seven hours on a single shore excursion or even a seven-day well-scripted vacation at a resort does not provide enough intel to make a life move. I was shocked to hear of people moving to Costa Rica because of a show they watched on HGTV. Rule number one if you can buy a home on the beach for less than a hundred thousand dollars, you probably shouldn't!

If the RAIN SEASON lasts several months and all the roads are made of dirt...RED FLAG. If there is a hunting season for the mosquitoes that are large enough to be mounted on your wall... RED FLAG. If there are only flights that leave the location on Thursday morning... RED

FLAG. If the local grocery store only gets a delivery on the first Tuesday of every month... RED FLAG. If 911 is you running two miles to the neighbors after an emergency... RED FLAG. If WIFI stands for What IF I get stuck in the mud....RED FLAG. If it takes on average a year and a half to sell a house there... RED FLAG.

In other words, make sure you think this through and that it aligns with your specific wants and desires. Economically and emotionally! If you want to live off the grid, move to where you can! If you want to live in the forest, to the mountains, or by the sea, move there! If you want sunshine all the time, move there! Take the time to think it through, write out what you are looking for, and get about finding it, then make the move! Life is short. Love yourself enough to live where YOU CHOOSE.

Now, let me address the "baby" elephant in the room. Some retirement-ready adults have not permitted themselves to leave the nest. Although we taught our children to be independent, many parents can't permit themselves to leave the very nest that they encouraged their offspring to leave.

Pre-retirement life was about raising the kids. We poured into our children. We made sure they had everything. We paid for their braces, coached them in sports, and made sure they got to go to Disneyland. We provided the character, and the foundation they needed to succeed.

Now, we have the freedom to pursue our best senior life! Most adult children will make it without us holding their hands and raising their children. You did, and yes, if both parents work and you are not offering free daycare for five or six years, this may impact the type of cars they drive or the home they live in. But, we should not feel guilty about living where we want, just as they won't hesitate to relocate if they have a better job opportunity.

Case Study – Bob and Betty moved from Seattle to Houston to be near their daughter, who moved there after college, married, and just had their first grandchild. Bob and Betty bought a house in the same Houston suburb as their daughter's family. One year later, their daughter got transferred to Chicago. The company sold the daughter's house at a loss and paid to move her family to Chicago. Bob now lives in Houston alone trying to sell that property, while Betty lives in an apartment in Chicago. Bob flies up once a month to visit. It will be a few years before Bob can sell the Houston house and join his family in ChiTown. This was not how they wanted to live out their retirement years!

One of my senior mantras... unless God says otherwise, "Don't follow the children." But, of course, there are exceptional circumstances. I am blessed with amazing siblings. One of my wonderful sisters, Teresa, is married to an exceptional man, Jim. Together, they have three children, one of whom has two sets of twins. TWO sets of twins. So, when deciding where they would retire, it made sense to move to the small town in Florida where their son Seth and his family lived. A set of 10-year-old girls and 3-year-old boys were more than enough to fill the household with challenges. Seth was also the pastor of a growing church with high demands on his and his wife's time. So, they felt compelled to move toward them and help add another layer of love and care for the grandchildren. They did not need to think long and hard over this. They did not need to put a GRID together; they needed to respond out of love for their family to the clear need.

This is where they want and need to be for the next decade, but it is a rare exception. After all, they also have a daughter in Tennessee with three kids of her own, a completely different situation with no compelling need to help. Therefore, it wasn't even a consideration to move there. The choice to move was not to empower a child to have a more significant lifestyle by providing free childcare for the grandchildren. Nor was it made because they felt guilty about their newfound freedom.

In my book **65 and Alive**!, I explain that when retiring, we need to do so with passion and purpose. We must find "a reason for living" that excites us to get up in the morning, off the couch, and out of the house. For many, it is a long-neglected hobby due to work obligations. For others, it is a ministry or charitable cause that they want to give more time. For others, it is finally traveling to all the places on their bucket list that they have put off until now.

It is also time to make the move to the place of our dreams. To finally get out of the rain, the smog, the snow, the humidity, the traffic. For some of us, it is to remove ourselves from a location of emotional pain or stress. To allow ourselves the freedom to start over, to reboot. To be FREE.

Most of us can honestly say we paid our dues. We raised our children and probably did a great job. Now we have permission, freedom, and the choice to move and LIVE where we will find joy and fulfillment. We have permission to move, travel and enjoy life. Whether it be Costa Rica or Cabo, Antarctica or Arkansas, love yourself enough to live where and how you find JOY and then visit the people you love with the high emotional energy that comes as a result. Everyone WINS! Take it from me, a self-proclaimed SENIORS EXPERT; permission granted!

And to those of you who are not ready to retire but ready to START OVER......give yourself permission to start somewhere NEW. Perhaps the time is now to get out of the rut you find yourself in and let go of letting others tell you why you should stay where you are and give yourself permission to reboot, restart, refresh, and renew. By making a MOVE to a new location you are opening up new thoughts, new relationships, and new opportunities. Due to most of us being able to work remotely, this opens up all kinds of possibilities, including living ABROAD! I know from my own life experience and having coached thousands to personal life success that in giving yourself permission to start somewhere new and then having the courage to make that move it can be one of the most freeing, self-loving things a human can do.

Author **Douglas Jessup**, founder of Coaching 4 Life Success, has been a motivational speaker and inspiring writer for the past twenty years. Author of five books, **8 Words 4 Life**, getting out of your rut and into real living! **They Call Me Coach**, How to develop the character of kids through youth sports. **65 and Alive!** How to Retire with Passion and Purpose. And International Best Seller **Why Mexico?:** The 7 Reasons I Retired in Cabo. He and his wife, Alma, live in Cabo San Lucas, Mexico. Together they run a non-profit, **Esperanza de Ninos**, providing hope and love, direction and protection for orphans living on the streets of Mexico, committed to the mission UNTIL EVERY CHILD HAS A HOME. They have four children and eight grandchildren.

You can find more on this subject by reading this author's latest book and #1 INTERNATIONAL BESTSELLER, **WHY MEXICO?: The 7 Reasons I Retired in Cabo https://a.co/d/jk2bt3d**

65 And Alive! https://a.co/d/1lp6PR6

Painting My Path: An Artistic Journey of Self-Love and Discovery

By Nathalie Villeneuve

"Until you make the unconscious conscious, it will direct your life, and you will call it fate." - Carl Jung.

We have different parts of ourselves, which are often kept secret or unnoticed. As Carl Jung wisely said, when we become aware of these hidden parts of ourselves, we can truly control our own future. We all have these distant parts that sometimes affect our decisions without realizing it.

A part of my early life was marked by a struggle with bedwetting, which made me feel different and ashamed. This experience left me feeling isolated and fearful, mainly as I tried to drift into sleep.

These emotions seemed too big for my age, a time when I should've been more carefree. I felt I didn't quite fit in and didn't understand why. This made me retreat into my world, trying to figure it all out. It was tough, like fighting a silent battle no one else could see.

I learned to pretend everything was normal, hiding my confusing feelings. Every day was challenging, but it made me strong, even if people didn't know what was happening. In my own unique way, I was a little warrior, trying to understand grown-up emotions while still being a child.

Discovering Self-Love Through Art

I found solace and discovered my love for creative expression at a young age. I remember the first week of school when our teacher asked us to draw circles using crayons, gouache, and colored pencils. It felt like Christmas.

As I effortlessly created near-perfect circles while others struggled, I realized for the first time I had a gift. It was subtle, but I held on to this feeling because I instinctively knew this was good for me. Drawing became my joyful escape, where I would sketch princesses, adorn them with sparkling glitter, and paint the sun in the most vibrant shade of yellow.

Every art project was like my bestie whispering a secret in my ear. Loving art so much allowed me to know myself a lot better. It's like having a magic mirror that shows who I truly am. Doing what I loved became a special game that helped me discover more fun stuff about myself. We don't connect those dots immediately as kids, but we have that special something inside us guiding our actions.

Using Art as a Healing Tool

At the age of ten, a teacher's request to design a poster for a class event became a turning point in my life. Art turned out to be more than just making pretty pictures. It became my way of dealing with tough times, like self-therapy. My sketchpad and the most available space in all my notebooks from school were my safe place, my personal haven, helping me make sense of my feelings.

Despite the ongoing issue of bedwetting, which had slowed down considerably even in my early teens, art was my go-to escape. Sure, the physical problem was highly irritating, but I turned to art to help me deal with it emotionally. It was my creative outlet, helping me deal with all the piled-up feelings.

Using art to understand my emotions led me to a path of self-love. Every line of a drawing or color was a step towards embracing myself. It reminded me that it's okay to have problems and be imperfect. The important thing is to love and accept myself as I am.

Art Becoming a Part of My Identity

My art supplies became my closest companions during my pre-teen years, often taking precedence over social interactions. I embraced the role of the introverted young artist who found a source of relief and consolation in the tranquility of drawing and painting.

My journals filled with sketches and drawings became a testament to my identity as an artist, a reflection of my journey towards self-love and acceptance.

Like many, I experienced moments when my passion and interests became integral to who I am, shaping my identity and providing a sense of purpose.

Bursting the Bubble of Self-Limitation

However, it's essential to recognize that finding comfort in a specific identity or lifestyle can sometimes limit potential. I vividly recall summoning the courage to step out of my comfort zone during my teenage years. I joined the gymnastics team, the diving team, and even the marching band. These experiences taught me the importance of breaking free from self-imposed boundaries and embracing new challenges. While my artistic pursuits provided comfort and security, exploring different avenues allowed me to grow and expand my horizons.

Personal growth often requires embracing discomfort and venturing beyond the familiar. At that time, I also knew I liked being independent, making my own decisions.

Enduring the Trials

These experiences exposed me to moments of self-doubt and a lack of confidence that lurked in the corners of my mind. Additionally, my struggle with secondary enuresis persisted; I was nervous at the thought of overnight gymnasium stays with numerous peers. Despite the challenging moments when I longed for familiarity and wished to retreat, I persevered, gradually navigating through those trials.

This trip was no walk in the park. But it gave me something special, something invaluable: a lesson in hanging tough. It emphasized that, even when things get rough, this strong, resilient part of us keeps pushing forward, no matter what.

It's a beautiful thing about being human, isn't it? We all come up against roadblocks, bumps in the road. But then we dig deep and somehow find the strength to press on.

And you know what's at the heart of that strength? It's self-love, mes amis.

Loving yourself enough to fight and keep going is the fuel that keeps our inner fire burning.

Self-Love as a Guide

Throughout these transformative experiences, self-love emerged as my guiding light, illuminating my path with authenticity and clarity.

With every accomplishment, every hurdle overcome, every brushstroke and performance, self-love became the empowering force that allowed me to thrive and unlock my true potential. It became the compass that directed me towards embracing my unique self, fostering self-compassion, and nurturing a deep appreciation for the person I was becoming.

This journey of self-love and discovery speaks to the universal longing for authenticity, self-acceptance, and personal growth within each of us.

The Power of Emotion and Self-Love

As I matured, I realized that suppressing my emotions hindered my ability to embrace self-love fully. I embarked on a journey of inviting self-love back into my life by acknowledging, accepting, and forgiving myself for my childhood condition.

The seeds of self-appreciation planted through my love for art began to flourish. I learned a great deal through reconnecting with my emotions and practicing self-compassion; I want to remind you that embracing our vulnerabilities, embracing all aspects of ourselves, and treating ourselves with kindness is integral to cultivating self-love.

Guiding Others Towards Self-Love Through Art

In recent years, I had the privilege of facilitating painting and creativity workshops, witnessing the transformative power of art firsthand. As I guided individuals step by step, their expressions and postures transformed, reflecting the emergence of self-love and newfound excitement for creative exploration.

These experiences reinforced the idea that art can catalyze self-discovery, empowering others to embrace their unique voices and navigate their own paths toward self-love.

Art-Journaling

I had to close up shop as the Pandemic put an abrupt interruption to facilitating workshops.

Wanting to continue my self-Love and healing journey, I have applied the magic of art journaling. It has become yet another powerful tool in navigating the valleys and peaks of life. No matter how much we grow, echoes of past traumas can linger, catching us off guard when we least expect it. Once again, art has proven to be a trusted ally, offering clarity and understanding and reinforcing self-love.

This art journaling practice motivated me to create coloring journals aimed at women so they can strive to become their best selves, nurture a deep connection, explore their own avenues of self-expression, and discover the transformative potential of art as a means of healing and self-love.

Navigating Boundaries and Cultivating Self-Love: An Invitation to Color Outside the Lines

Honoring our uniqueness and authenticity can't be overstated in a world that often confines us within predetermined boxes. It's essential to unchain ourselves from external expectations, unfurl our wings, and revel in the beauty of our individuality.

An Invitation to Embrace Self-Love

This is an invitation to us to courageously break free from these societal confines and joyfully engage in the art of coloring outside the lines of our own lives. It's time to take the brush, choose colors, and create vibrant masterpieces!

This narrative is more than just my story; it invites you to embark on your journey of self-discovery and self-love. Recognize the beauty in your uniqueness and let your passions fuel your journey. Remember that the strength to overcome challenges, foster self-acceptance, and celebrate your unique existence lies within you.

Painting My Path: An Artistic Journey of Self-Love and Discovery
By Nathalie Villeneuve

Nathalie Villeneuve is on a transformative mission, empowering women worldwide to embrace their innate creativity and fearlessly color outside the lines.

Her meticulously crafted journals and captivating coloring books create a sanctuary of creativity, providing a cathartic escape and a profound outlet for self-discovery.

Beyond her writing, Nathalie's artistic prowess spans various disciplines, including painting, fashion, graphic design, home staging, and workshop facilitation.

This diverse background enriches her creative mentorship, enabling her to guide individuals on their unique journeys of self-expression with depth and wisdom.

Through every brushstroke, Nathalie breathes life into her work, recognizing that art transcends mere visual splendor—it becomes a conduit for capturing the depths of human emotions and experiences.

Join Nathalie on a transformative artistic odyssey, exploring her captivating creations on her Amazon author's page, seeking inspiration from her curated YouTube playlist, or connecting with her vibrant creative community on LinkedIn.

Remember, you can also own one of Nathalie's breathtaking paintings or commission an extraordinary piece directly from her website at nathalievilleneuve.com. Let Nathalie Villeneuve infuse your heart with emotion through her masterful strokes, and watch your creativity soar to new heights.

Website: NathalieVilleneuve.com

Linktree: linktr.ee/pauseandpaint

Facebook: facebook.com/NathalieDVilleneuve/

Author's Page: amazon.com/author/nathalievilleneuve

Abandoned Thoughts

By Shaun Brefo

"They left me!" I woke up in the darkness and then realized I was alone. I ran room to room in a frenzy, looking around the house to see if anyone was home. At four years old, I was just tall enough to open the front door but not enough to turn on the lights or open the front gate outside our Houston apartment.

I rushed outside and peeked through the fence to see if my parents' cars were home. After noticing they were gone, I went back inside to check the rooms one more time before throwing my body on the couch. Sobbing, I punched the pillow and muttered, "I can't trust anyone, not even my family. I've gotta find my own way." My first abandonment shaped me into someone who listened to people deeply and made sure people felt seen and heard.

I set out on a journey to truly know myself. For the most part, I grew up a pretty quiet kid. I was born in a little country town in Illinois, so I was teased in grade school for saying things like "pop" instead of "Coke." I made good grades and didn't give my parents that big of a hassle. I grew up without grandparents on either side, leaving my busy mom and dad to do all the work of raising four boys.

I felt like I was the most ambitious of my siblings. I was always willing to try something new to get ahead. I wanted to change everything for my family, financially, mentally, etc. So much to the point that I started to pride myself on being different from my siblings. I was the first to leave home and attend a big-name University.

I had my own set of traumas, as we all do in elementary, middle, and high school, but nothing too big to discourage me from trying to be the best I could be. From verbal bullying to being abandoned by the people who were supposed to love me the most, the tough parts of life really started to set in.

After being molested by a young neighbor boy, I got into porn at a young age, which escalated to male-on-male porn and became my little secret. I swore I would never tell anyone because it was who I was behind closed doors. I hid this secret pretty well throughout most of high school and definitely in college. I went to a pretty conservative University where I later learned that there were a handful of students there exploring their sexuality. It was called "Closet Station" in the gay community because most of the gay community was closeted or "not out to the public."

I was SO closeted I hid it from myself. Almost like a lie, I would tell myself, "It's okay. It's just a phase." I knew my actions made me a non-heterosexual, but I kept acting like it was not me or a dream. I abandoned a part of myself in the process. The fear of judgment and being abandoned if people knew who I really was behind closed doors left me very surface-level and partially inauthentic.

The pornography got really out of hand in my Senior year of college with late nights and not being productive. I decided to do something about it and committed to going one year without pornography. I made it 11 months before a viewing that wasn't in my control, but in integrity, I ended my challenge. I was extremely proud of myself. I had severed the chain pornography had on me, thus taking away its power and control over me.

After a personal development seminar in Los Angeles to grow my business, I finally got honest with myself. I released a bunch of pinned-up emotions about my parents and family trauma. It allowed me to truly forgive them for past hurts. On one of the follow-up calls with a team leader after the event, I had a sudden urge to say it. I was also scared of being shamed by the young lady who showed me nothing but overwhelming support for being courageous and "coming out" to her.

It came to me like an epiphany after the phone call, "Oh shit, I'm gay." I bawled my eyes out the whole drive back to Houston from California. The fear of judgment, the fear of not being enough for my family, and the fear of not having a family one day all hit me like a ton of bricks. So many fears arose in me that day, but I was finally honest with myself. The fear was still pretty crippling. Through all the suppressed emotions over the years being released in the event, my vision was finally clear enough to see who I was. I still wasn't ready to share this with the world.

That is when the journey began. The Journey of learning to love what was, both my family and myself, and not being afraid of who I really was. It was not always smooth and easy... As I look back on the path that I've traveled, it feels like I have literally been peeling back an onion. Tears have been shed, and there have been moments of triumph and fear resurfacing. I can remember nights centered in shame, guilt, and trying to figure out who I was without simply ignoring it like I used to. I had to remember I was on a journey of self-discovery and getting closer to truly falling in love with who I was. I would accept and not abandon myself.

Once I started to accept who I was, I began to break through to a deeper level of knowing myself and starting to realize my patterns and triggers around my emotions. I first came out as Bisexual on Facebook because I did have some fun times with women. In my mind, I believed it was more acceptable to be bi than gay.

As time progressed, I learned more about myself, dated more women, and wondered why the relationships could not last for more than a month. I was messing around with guys outside of my relationships but dating women who couldn't keep my interest for one reason or another. I was not in alignment with these women.

Another coach I've recently started working with said something powerful after I came out to him. He said, "Shaun, I know I don't know you that well, but you're an amazing guy, and you've done a lot for many people. If you truly want to step into the most powerful, authentic version of yourself, you get to OWN WHO YOU ARE. Make a declaration of whatever the hell you want and choose it powerfully, and you will watch the world unfold to give you what you want." At that moment, it all made sense. I was so focused on what I felt I should, must, or needed to have because of societal pressures that I totally stepped over and even forgot about the things that lit me up, made me feel alive, and brought the most happiness to my life.

I realized an important lesson. This is an ongoing Journey. It took being 100% honest with myself and deciding to trust the process. The process of learning to trust myself, my decisions, and who I am as an individual. It's not easy, but it's worth it to live fully expressed and not feel like I must be something for someone else. I want to be myself wholeheartedly. It's an amazing experience. I have never been a huge fan of labels. I never felt like everyone had to know who I was or who I liked, but to feel that I could be myself, unapologetically is so freeing.

Those tears cried on the way home from Los Angeles, California, released me. Although it's still a journey every day, every month, and every year, I trust myself now more than ever, and I'm proud of what I have become. It has made me a problem solver because I want to have kids one day. Regardless of who I end up with, they are gonna be one lucky son of a bitch, because I decided to stop beating myself up and took ownership after accepting myself.

The journey to self-love happens every day. My plea to you as you explore yourself in whatever capacity to become the best version of yourself is to live authentically and be patient with yourself. Trust the process, and love yourself through it because no one gets out of this life alive. Embrace the Journey. My journey is far from ending. Whenever I feel like new emotions are surfacing, I remind myself it's just part of the journey. Then, I embrace it.

I have abandoned my self-doubt and my closets, self-imposed and societal. I abandon all that does not serve me and embrace all that I am.

Shaun Brefo went from managing organizations of salespeople to a lifestyle coach. One conversation with Shaun shows why he was meant to heal souls, habits, and triggers holding you back from being fully unleashed in your life. Succeeding in sales and building top sales organizations in the door-to-door world and recently in the life insurance industry, Shaun gracefully leads people to be the leader in their own life, trust their intuition, and be the change they want to see in the world. Shaun "Coach Brefo" now runs SKB Quantum Consulting, where he helps entrepreneurs and business owners shift their personality to create a new personal reality and live the life they deserve.

Shaun not only has an infectious smile, but he has also made it his mission to see a smile on every face he sees.

Shaun is a living, breathing mountain of love. His ease of connection is due to his kind, compassionate nature and bedrock of strength for others if they feel messy.

Simply put, Shaun lives and embodies the joy, happiness, and love needed to help people transform their lives.

Abandoned Thoughts
By Shaun Brefo

SKB Quantum Consulting LLC

Instagram @Coachbrefo

Fb.com/coachbrefo

Love Stream

By Kenya Evelyn

I started believing that I deserved the love I had always dreamed of.

It was a hot summer day. I woke up early with the kids and got ready. I was about to experience being under waterfalls for the first time in my life. It was a pleasant drive, about 2 hours from home, with dark greens on both sides of the road, blue sky, and deep conversation. The friend that instigated this trip was a match made in heaven.

I parked the car and went to buy our tickets. My daughter started playing with a plush toy rattlesnake. Oh No! Are there snakes here? Something in me questioned my decision to step into this adventure.

I remembered intention holds the calibration of the event. The calibration will define if my brain records the event as positive or negative. Something my nervous system will lean towards it or avoid it at all costs.

My intention was to bathe under the waterfalls. The potential of a rattlesnake on the state park could have lowered my calibration or taken me out of the game completely, but I chose the breakthrough of the first moment in time, and God showed up as a spiritual experience and love in overflow. I got to practice setting intentions. I breathed in what I want more of, and trusted that it was so.

I looked at the map that turned out to be of zero help. The trails to get to the falls weren't in it. It was a long hike in the dirt and an even longer beside the streams to get to the bottom of the falls. The rocks were so big and slippery and simultaneously stunningly beautiful. Every step was a new challenge, a new picture, and a new invitation to love.

Being in nature pulls me closer to God and becomes the greatest expression of self-love when I am grounded and can hear the voices within by just BEeing.

How many times have I avoided time for myself?

When was the last time I did something that felt like play or got lost in something out of sheer joy? Five years ago, I couldn't have answered if I had been asked.

I came from a long lineage of women that believed that selflessness was the way to be. I was taught giving was better than receiving. Giving like this can lead to resentment and emptiness after a while. My soul wanted to give from Love.

I see now that loving others as I love myself is THE MAP that works every time. It's a map of resonance. No one can love me more than I love myself. It is and always will be a frequency match.

As I walked the slippery rocks to get to my "waterfalls of a promised land," falling a few times and getting bruised, I noticed the sound of the stream was getting louder. We were getting closer. I surrendered to the moment and allowed the time to freeze. I enjoyed watching my daughter believe she was a mermaid and added that memory to my childhood collection. I let my concerns and frustrations quiet and loved this moment.

The most extraordinary love story I can have is the one where I am in tune with myself, my needs, my mission, my vision, and my being. Delighting myself in me, soaking in my love for me, and taking pleasure that flows at the heart of everything.

I have wanted someone to love me my entire life. I had so many rules about it, which made it conditional. Even worse, I made rules my husband didn't even know existed. At the same time, I had so many rules for when I would and could love myself. Only when I decided I was worthy of having it all did my husband show up for me. He met me at the level of interdependency, intimacy, love, and celebration I held for myself. My internal conversation became I accept, I deserve, I allow.

The way I see myself is the way the world will see me. Experiencing THIS truth was a defining moment.

The day I realized this was "The special day"—my wedding with myself. The secret of having it all was the moment I decided to put a mirror on myself and take care of my own needs.

I re-established that connection with myself. I claimed my sovereignty, autonomy, and my leadership. I set the tone.

In my body,

In my heart,

In my soul,

I am ready to share, by overflow, with the world. Just like waterfalls.

The best adventure of my life was the decision to love me just as I am.

I started to experience the delicious flavor of every moment as is.

When I finally set myself under the waterfalls, I felt a spiritual experience of an overwhelming weight of blessings, abundance, and love filling up my cup. Can I receive this much? Yes, I can!

I was silent for a long time while my daughter begged me to return to the bottom of the falls to swim in the natural pool. I was mesmerized by the perfection of this moment of so much love, so much water, so much intention, so much joy!

In my health coaching training, I recalled that we are made of 70% water. Water is who we are. Water is life. Water is the carrier of all things good in our bodies—just like love. I don't have love. I am love. The miracle of alignment in self-love is that loving, accepting, and embracing every part of me makes me whole and complete. Every motion and e-motion that shows up as me is welcomed. I honor my voice and my desires. I believe in every possibility for me because nothing is outward, and I know who I am.

I noticed that the current was so heavy when I was underneath the falls that it almost took me to the next layer of it. What a great metaphor! When I love myself and surrender to the current of love, it carries me to the next level, where I love others from my overflow. All my success in every area comes from how much I love myself. And

228

through my alignment and my desires comes my voice. So, my mission is to love myself even more.

How many times have I blocked love because I felt undeserving?

How often did I misinterpret it because the voice of trauma came out faster than me? How many times have I thought and spoken in the tone of judgment or self-hatred, not mattering and not voicing my desires?

Today I feel, hear, smell, taste, and know that I am deserving. I hold the codes of unconditional love, abundance, and miracles.

I could believe self-love was taking a bubble bath, having my hair done, or anything that showed I cared for myself. Sometimes this is the *activity* I need at that moment. The deeper self-love is within. Self-love is "the work." It is an internal job. I had to stop the noise and take time to listen as God's daughter. I had to step back into the frequency of miracles, freedom, abundance, and truth.

I choose a life led by desire, possibility, and gratitude because I love first what is and whatever else shows up. This love carries every cell of my body in the past, present, and future.

I have been magnetically pulled to ho'oponopono in the past three years.

Ho'oponopono is a practice of loving yourself enough to let go and make space for what is for you.

I love you -I am sorry -Forgive me -Thank you

Our souls receive the words as a fresh breeze of letting go of what doesn't serve and welcoming the new, not allowing anyone or any situation to consume you.

Many say that ho'oponopono is a forgiveness practice. I see it as deep self-love and a way to keep your " house clean."

I invite you to celebrate yourself and the world that is created out of you. Play, pray, sing, dance, swim, and be in joy.

You are a gift.

You are a miracle, unique and perfect.

I invite myself to remember the Ho'oponopono and the waterfall's weight and cleansing nature. I invite myself to remember my daughter playing freely from a place of unconditional love. I invite myself to stay in the Love Stream.

With Deep Love,

Kenya

As a gift to you, you can download my recording of ho'oponopono as a song on my website. Kenyaevelyn.com

Kenya Evelyn lives in Nashville, TN with her three kids and husband of seventeen years. She is passionate about God, her family and awakening the truth of our light and the power of our being. A lifelong singer and certified music therapist, energy healer, health coach and life coach, she is a powerful Intuitive Frequency Alchemist. She teaches others how to harmonize their energy, vibration and frequency to achieve a life of fulfillment, celebrating and purpose—what she calls *wealth*— through aligned frequency. Kenya believes in creating stronger families and supporting women who love themselves so unconditionally that everything they touch is calibrated with the frequency of abundance, sovereignty and autonomy. She creates with ease and flow; hosts retreats, masterminds and singing circles; provides one-on-one coaching; facilitates "Night of Healing" and "Frequency Codes". She invites you to reclaim your voice, find your rhythm, learn your frequencies, discover your divine design and amplify your power through voice and movement.

www.kenyaevelyn.com

https://www.facebook.com/kenya.evelyn.7/

Love Stream
By Kenya Evelyn

https://www.instagram.com/frequency.alchemist/

The Goddess Within

By Meeka Caissie

"You look like a Goddamn sausage in those jeans. Go change!" He hollered. I was 13. Looking back, I know my Dad wasn't calling me fat, ugly, unloveable, or not enough, but that is what I heard. I ran to my room to change my clothes, yelling and screaming.

I wasn't the smartest one in class, I wasn't on any winning sports teams, I wasn't the prettiest, and I didn't 'put out.' I needed those spray-on jeans that everyone was wearing, or I wouldn't have any friends. I stacked that story with many others to build a strong case that I wasn't loveable and I definitely wasn't enough.

School was not my happy place. I was bullied terribly, and after attending 11 of them, I quit, not once, but twice. I ran away from home at 17 after finding my Dad in bed with someone who wasn't my Mom. I moved to the next big city, Montreal, where I met a very kind and compassionate lady who took me in for a couple of weeks until I found work and secured a tiny apartment of my own. I lied about my age to get a bartending job. I quickly discovered the more makeup I put on, the fewer clothes I wore, and the higher my heels, the more tips I made. My fellow bartenders taught me in the staff restroom how to stuff my bra with socks and put contoured makeup on my tiny cleavage to make my breasts look bigger. They outlined my lips with lip liner and told me, "Clients love pouty lips."

We flirted, starved, and drank with customers to make money to pay our rent and, more importantly, keep our hair, nails, lashes, etc., paid for. I lost a piece of myself in that bar. Do you remember where you lost a piece of yourself?

Fast forward a few years, and there I was with breast implants, an eating disorder, movie makeup, highlights in my hair, extensions on my nails and eyelashes, eyebrows painted, teeth whitened and capped, lips plumped and glossed, botox-filled wrinkles, brand labeled clothes, shoes, bags, a fancy car, fancy home and photos of it all through ring lights and phone filters. Am I enough now? Now will they love me? Can you relate? When will it stop? How did this happen? Do you remember your first 'enhancement'? Who you were with, and why did you do it? Was it to belong? Was it to fit in or to ease the pain of not feeling enough? Is it working?

Is that what we want? Is that what we believe the men want? Or are we doing it for each other? I often wonder, as women, are we perpetuating the race to 'beauty/youth'? Are we competing? I remember reading, 'Girls compete against each other, Women empower each other.' Don't you love that?! Are we the ones actually creating the issue for the next generation? Are we teaching men (and our sons and daughters) what lovable looks like? Are we role modeling for our kids that they aren't enough as they are? That their physical beauty defines their future happiness? Are we defining ourselves through filters, plastic surgery, and injections? Is that how we measure our self-worth and our value in the world? Is that healthy? I remember my Mom saying, "Do as I say, not as I do " I love you more than anyone, Mom, but that didn't always work lol

I thought my breast implants would bring me confidence and make me feel sexier and more loveable, and they did for about 5 minutes. All they did was attract a kind of *love* as real as the silicone bags themselves. Then I began to hate myself, obsess about a wrinkle, a spot, a pound. I lost me, I lost my value, and I lost touch with the magical, beautiful, warm heart and shine I bring. Have you?

Imagine for a moment, if you would, falling in love with yourself in all of your natural glory. Slowly allowing the Botox to dissolve, the nails to fall off, the colour to fade, loving yourself enough to eat to live, exercising not to be slim but rather to thrive and build vitality. Know that your zest for life, kindness, compassion, smile, creativity, leadership, great listening skills, or great storytelling skills make you so special. BEing unapologetically and authentically you. We teach people how to treat us. Please take that into your heart. We teach people how to treat us. It's time to raise your standards and realize YOU are enough. It's time to shine.

Are we doing all this to attract a life partner or lover? Friends? Are we doing it to find love? Or in an effort to love ourselves? Do we blame the men? They won't love me unless I _____. Or do we blame the women? They won't accept me unless I _____. Is this how we build rapport now, through Botox and lashes? When did we buy in that we are not enough as we are? When did we accept to be seen and loved, we must look like others (or ourselves ten years ago)?

What if we were already shining? I mean, really shining. Shining our love, compassion, authentic smile, and a body that says I am living my life fully and with expression. ***This is me!*** How can we be trusted if we pretend to be someone we are not? What is under curtain #1? At what point will we heal the story and change the story? As Tony Robbins says, "Change your story, change your life." Confidence is a habit, just as loving yourself and living with joy is a habit. This is what I love most about what happens at my retreats, healing, transformation, compassion, love, joy, and celebration in just days of full immersion.

Whether you love yourself or someone else, is it based on *purchased* beauty? How deep can that love go, and how long can it last? Will it ever be enough? Will you? Is it time to explore that? You are a miracle, and your miraculous body will always wonder "***why***"?

"Why" do you not believe the statement, I am enough? Why do you not caress and adore me as I am? I gave you everything, a beating heart to love and to be loved. Eyes to see all the beauty around us and to pierce another person's soul with our gaze. I gave you a smile to bring light to someone's darkness, breasts to comfort, nourish and give life. I gave you legs to walk and arms to lift. When will you choose to be happy with ME and be grateful for all you are, and for all we've been given.

I imagine, our bodies are desperately seeking to know this. Thank God, my Mom role modeled resilience, forgiveness, and strength—all the virtues I've needed to help me change my story and change my life. I am grateful for the journey to loving myself botox and silicone free!

You, my friend, are God's highest form of creation. You are enough. You matter, and yes, I love you, AND what's most powerful is when YOU love you. It may take practice, tears, and forgiveness, and that is ok, one step at a time. You will get there, one breath at a time. **I believe in you! I am cheering for you! It's your time to shine!**

Meeka Caissie

Speaker, Transformational Therapist & Coach

DiamondGirls.ca

Speaker, Transformational Therapist & Coach

Meeka is a passionate, no-nonsense risk-taker and lover of life. With personal mentoring from legends like Bob Proctor, Julio Iglesias, and Tony Robbins, she is driven to leave this world better than before she came into it, one person at a time. After more than 20 years working in the entertainment industry and overcoming infertility, body dysmorphia, and loss of identity, she has great compassion and deeply connects with her clients helping them heal, step into their greatness, raise their standards, and get after their goals now!

As a certified coach and counselor who has experienced her own healing journey and thousands of others, Meeka wakes up every day eager to serve, whether from the stage, in one of her intimate retreats, or one-on-one. She uplifts, empowers, motivates change, finds your blind spots, and says what you need to hear, not just what you want to hear. She believes in you when you don't. Her energy is contagious, and you will often hear her say, "It's your time to raise your standards. It's time to shine!"

The Afterword

It has been less than ninety days since I decided to do a small book project on self-love before a light summer with my son in our new home. After a fascinating and complicated two years, I decided to take some time to work on our home, myself, and our new property.

I love working with authors. I love words and the value of a small nugget of gold from each human I meet. I decided to work only with authors I had published with before to make it nice and easy for all of us, and our nugget would be on what Self Love means to each of us.

Along the way, a few of my favorite authors introduced me to a new incredible people, and in only a few weeks, we had the authors selected for My Two Cents on Self-Love, the collection you have just completed. It all seems so seamless.

The book became a pivotal part of my own journey. Just over a month before our exciting launch date, my life changed forever. My son passed away in our home one morning after a stroke.

This experience has been more in-depth than I could have imagined, even after helping others through the grief cycle for almost twenty years. This is where Grief showed me clarity on how to help others even more and help myself through something heavier than anything before.

I will see the one-month anniversary of Hayden Ray's passing in a few days. I am lost. I am dazed. I am confused. And I am loved, supported, and cared for!

This book and the chapters held within are how and why I was able to re-enter society. My commitment to self-love includes loving this new piece of me just as I would love a scar or blemish. I love the part of me that has experienced grief. I honor this part of me. I support this part of me, and because I know I can trust Me to take care of myself without excuse or exception, my grief is allowing me to love in this space.

Self-love isn't always the fun part. It is the part that changes everything. It is my superpower.

We, collectively and individually, appreciate your support of this project!

I appreciate your support more than I can say, which is saying a lot, as I always have something to say about how I love ME!

Until next time.

I love you.

I love me.

I see you.

I hear you.

I am you.

Keep writing, Mistilei

Made in United States
Troutdale, OR
08/23/2023

12327330R00139